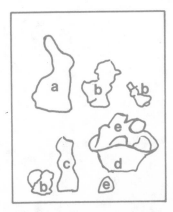

Cover photo:
a-b-c. Solid Easter Pieces 20
d. Basket 21
e. Marzipan Strawberries 48

Adventures in Cooking SERIES

how to make CANDY

Catherine Wagner

Illustrations by Laura Cave

Culinary Arts Institute®

Contents

Delair Publishing Company, Inc.
420 Lexington Avenue,
New York, New York 10170

Manufactured in the United States of America and published simultaneously in Canada.

ISBN: 0-8326-0637-5

Introduction

Have you ever gone somewhere you didn't particularly feel like going and wound up glad you went? Well, that is what happened to me in November of 1977. My sister invited me to attend a candy class with her. Attending that class was the last thing in the world I wanted to do but "Beady" assured me the class was scheduled to last only two hours. So, I agreed to go with her. Mentally, however, I was convinced there was **no one** who could possibly teach **me** how to make chocolate-covered cherries, peanut butter cups, creams, French mints, or any of the other delicious varieties available in the gift-wrapped boxes at the local drugstore, or in the candy department of the major department stores in the nearest city.

As it turned out, that two hour class changed my whole life. The teacher made it all seem so simple, I decided to go home and try it. Voilá! It wasn't that I couldn't do it; it was just that I had never been taught how. That has to be it—because, exactly one week later, using my standard kitchen equipment, for the most part I was making professional candy and giving it as Christmas gifts. I found out later that some of the recipients of my homemade gift hid their box of candy to make the treasure last a little longer.

Living in a rural area, the word got out that I could make candy. People began asking me if I'd consider making the candy to sell. My hus-band and I talked it over and by Easter the whole family was up to its eyeballs in chocolate. A local scout troop took on selling our candy as a way to raise money and we were kept busy turning out solid rabbits, filled (that is, fruit and nut, maple nut, etc.) eggs, novelty lollipops, chocolate baskets filled with chocolates and other holiday items.

I'm now convinced that anyone could do the same thing. As a result of that conviction, I decided to write this book. I originally planned to share what I've learned about making profes-sional looking and tasty candy in my own home, but as I began talking about my project, friends and family encouraged me to go beyond the original plans and include traditional home recipes.

We spent many hours reminiscing about the candy we used to make on Sunday afternoons. Mother had one certain cooking pot (and she still has the same old cooking pot today) we always used. We'd cook the sugar, milk, cocoa and salt, test in a cup of cold water for a soft ball, add the butter, (and maybe a little peanut butter) beat and pour. Then the wait would begin. Sometimes it got hard and we'd cut and enjoy it; but, sometimes, alas and alack, something went haywire and the eleven of us would sit with spoons and eat it that way—enjoying the chocolaty sweetness just the same.

And so, this book is designed in two sections—one dealing with professional type candy and the other dealing with the kinds of candy we remember as homemade candy.

As you peruse the pages of the first section, I hope you'll feel as I did and adopt the attitude that it's not that you can't do it, it's just that no one has ever shown you how and try your hand at chocolates. Using the method I've outlined, it's not difficult. Believe me

As you look over the second section, I hope a recipe or two will stir a memory for you and maybe one Sunday afternoon you'll make candy with your kids, too. Memories are made of this.

My hope is that you will enjoy reading this book, enjoy reminiscing, enjoy trying the various recipes, and most of all, enjoy eating the candy.

Have fun!
Cathy

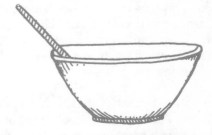

Supplies, Ingredients and Equipment

Supplies and Ingredients

Cherries

Candied. These are dried cherries to which a sweetener has been added. They are extremely sweet to the taste and are sticky in appearance. This type of cherry is used when adding cherries to fondant—such as fruit and nut eggs or cherry-nut centers. Available in red and green, they can be found at Christmas time in grocery stores and some "5 & 10's". They are available year round at large candy and bakery supply houses.

Maraschino. These are the cherries, available in both red and green, which come packaged in a can or jar of liquid. They are readily found in grocery stores and come with or without stems. This type of cherry is used in chocolate covered cherries.

Maraschino cherries can be substituted for candied cherries in most recipes; however, they must be air-dried for six weeks first.

Chocolate

Coating. (Known as molding candy or summer coating.) This is a special type of chocolate used for molding and coating candy. In addition to the standard chocolate flavor, it is available in white, pink, yellow, and green which have a vanilla flavor, as well as tan, which is both butterscotch and peanut butter flavored. I recommend the use of coating chocolate because of its success rate. The few simple steps of preparation make the product a joy to work with and the resulting smooth confection is a taste treat. In addition, when compared to pure milk chocolate, coating chocolate is very economical to use. It is also a product which can be remelted in the oven.

Pure Milk. This ingredient contains cocoa butter and *must be tempered* before using. The recipes in this book can be used with either type of chocolate. Neither of these chocolates can tolerate even one drop of water as it will cause them to gel. This includes water-based flavorings and dyes. Flavoring oils and paste food colors do the job nicely.

Coconut

Angel Flake. This is a moist, thin string coconut often used in home cooking. This type of coconut can be purchased from a grocery store. It is usually sweetened.

Macaroon. This is a more natural kind of coconut, this has been dried and grated into pieces. Often dark specks appear in the coconut. These are minute pieces of shell and should be no cause for alarm. The coconut is *not* dirty.

Bon-bons and coconut clusters are examples of candies using macaroon coconut. It is available from candy and bakery supply houses.

Coloring

Liquid. This type of coloring is fine for fondants. It comes in four colors: red, blue, yellow and green. They can be combined to create other shades. These have a water base and can be found on the grocer's shelf.

Paste. This somewhat thick coloring comes in small jars. Any type of chocolate should be colored only with paste food colors. (As mentioned before, any liquid will cause chocolate to gel.) Since chocolate already comes in a variety of colors, one may need only a few jars of coloring to change or darken a color.

The colors are very concentrated. If paste colors become thick in the jar, add a drop or two of glycerin and stir.

Paste is available individually in a wide selection of colors or in kits containing the basic colors. Candy or bakery supply houses usually stock this product.

Flavoring

Extracts. Water based flavorings, available in grocery stores, are known as extracts. This type of flavoring is especially recommended for fondants, cream centers, and homemade candies.

Oils. These are very strong flavorings which do not contain water. In addition to candy and cake supply outlets, they are usually available in drug stores. These come in small, one dram bottles and are sometimes referred to as "hard candy" flavorings. This is the only type of flavoring which can be used in coating or milk chocolate. Oil based flavoring can be used in fondants; however, due to the concentration, one should only use a few drops per pound of fondant.

Fondants

Creamy White. This is a creamy base of a piece of candy which has the appearance of a creamy paste. It is available commercially and known as ready-made fondant. However, the recipe for this type of fondant is included in the Homemade Candy section of this book.

Creamy White Fondant is unflavored; therefore, you must add extracts and food coloring to make your favorite creams. Often it is somewhat stiff when purchased but can be made creamy by kneading.

Dry. A basic sugar substance which has the appearance of powdered sugar. This product is used especially for making chocolate covered cherries. Dry fondant can also be reconstituted into a cream for use in a piece of candy with a cream center. This type of cream is somewhat sweeter than most creams. One advantage of using dry fondant for a cream center is a better control over consistency. This, too, is available from candy supply houses.

Fruit

Candied. For general description, usage, and availability, see *Candied Cherries* above.

Fresh. Fresh or canned fruit can be dipped in a chocolate fondue or coated with chocolate but the shelf life is very short, three days maximum, and the sooner the product is consumed, the better.

Milk

Evaporated. This is unsweetened, concentrated milk which has been reduced to half or less of its bulk by evaporation. It is packed in cans.

Fresh. Found in the dairy case, fresh milk comes as skim, 2%, or whole milk. The difference is in the butterfat content. They are interchangeable in recipes calling for milk.

Sweetened Condensed. This is a cream colored, thick, very sweet milk. Care should be taken not to confuse this with evaporated milk as this also comes in cans. Both evaporated and sweetened condensed milk can be found on the grocer's shelf. Both should be in the same area.

Nuts

Nuts, which are used in making candy, can be

either salted or unsalted. Care should be taken not to pour salted nuts from the bag into the melted chocolate as the excess salt in the bottom of the bag will go into the chocolate, causing it to become distasteful.

Paramount Crystals
This is a type of vegetable oil. It has the appearance of small clear crystals and is used to thin chocolate if the chocolate seems too thick after it has been melted.

Equipment
Brushes
A fine tipped brush is required for painting molds while a slightly wider brush, approximately ¼″ or .62 centimeters, is used for making the outer shell of a cream center piece of candy or chocolate covered cherry. I recommend a good quality brush, one which will not tend to lose its hairs.

Clips
Clips are used to fasten the sections of a two-piece mold while it is being used. While small clips, spring type clothespins, and paper clips will hold a mold together, they are not strong enough to prevent a little melted chocolate from leaking through the clamped area. Thus, it becomes necessary to trim the excess ridge of candy after it has hardened and been removed from the mold. Medium binder clips are strong enough to do the job, yet not so large that they are awkward. They are easy to find in supply shops, "5 & 10's", hardware stores, and candy supply houses.

Dipping Fork
Bon-bon. Using a dipping fork eliminates the mess from hand dipping. The bon-bon dipping fork, used in candy making, resembles a hollow spoon. It is used for dipping large pieces of candy, fruit, or marshmallows.

Swirl. The swirl dipping fork has a coiled spoon area. While this fork is used mainly to dip smaller items such as candy, nuts, and broken pretzels, it is also used to put a design on a piece

of candy after it has been dipped.
Dipping forks can be purchased from candy and bakery supply houses; however, they are not an absolute necessity for the recipes in this book. A kitchen dinner fork will serve this purpose.

Fluted Paper Cups
Available from the candy and bakery supply shops, these are not a necessity but do make a box or plate of candy look "finished" and more professional. They are usually less expensive in large quantities. Ask about prices.

Funnel
A funnel and a wooden stopper or control rod is used to help regulate the flow of melted candy coating, fondant, or hard candy. This is only a convenience item and not a necessity. Mints can be dropped from a spoon and hard candy can be poured onto a greased cookie sheet. Candy funnels are available at larger candy supply houses.

Glass Jars and Plates
Baby food jars are ideal for storing individual colored candy wafers. These wafers are sold in most candy supply shops. They should be

separated immediately and stored in the baby food jars; otherwise they may melt into each other.

A glass pyrex plate or vegetable bowl is ideal for melting chocolate in the oven.

Heating Surfaces

Unless chocolate is used quickly after melting, a warm surface is needed to prevent the candy coating from rehardening. Here are a few suggestions: a warming tray, hot water bottle, heating pad, or electric skillet. Keep the surface warm enough only to keep the chocolate melted. If the warming surface is too warm to touch, it's too warm for the dish of candy.

Measuring Cups

To assure smooth and extremely good tasting candy, it is very important to measure the ingredients accurately. I recommend the use of measuring cups in graduated sizes.

Molds

Clear Plastic. For the professional look in candy making, molds are a necessity. Chocolate candy molds are plastic and need very little care for they are pre-treated to prevent the candy from sticking. Molds need not be cleaned after each use but only at the end of each season. To clean, simply wash under warm water and dry. (Do not clean in dishwasher or put near intense heat.)

Molds for coating chocolate are available in two types:

Flat. These give candy a design on the front of a piece only; the bottom is flat.

Two-Piece. These are used to make a chocolate item with a design on the back and front. They are usually used for solid chocolate pieces such as rabbits or santas or for chocolate baskets.

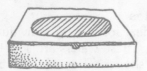

Rubber Mats

A rubber mat can be purchased from a hardware or department store. It should have narrow ridges and be approximately 12″ x 18″ (30 cm. x 45 cm.). This is used for dropped hot fondant and the result is a wafer with ridges across the back.

Rubber Molds

These are usually purchased in a yellow strip of five shapes or a single shape in a gray mold. Fancy mints can be made using these pre-shaped molds. They are available in many shapes for all occasions. Although this type of mold is designed especially for cream cheese mints, they can also be used for molding melted coating chocolate and sugar.

Metal Molds

Metal molds are used primarily for making hard candy suckers or molded hardtack pieces. These molds are somewhat expensive and can be found in larger candy supply shops. They usually contain three or less cavities; therefore, several molds are needed if you are planning to utilize the entire batch of candy made from the hard candy recipe included in this book.

Aluminum Molds. To prevent the hard candy syrup from sticking, this type of metal mold must be coated with vegetable oil before using. No special care is required for storing this type of mold.

Tin Molds. These molds also require a coating of vegetable oil before using. To prolong the life of these molds, after each use, they must be brushed with vegetable oil before storing.

Sucker Sticks

Sucker sticks are made of rolled paper to insure safety to children. Although they are used primarily for making lollipops, they are sometimes utilized for "painting" molds. Candy and bakery supply shops are outlets for purchasing this item.

Thermometers

A candy thermometer is used to measure the temperature of your cooked, homemade candy.

Preparing the Chocolate Coating

Preparing the chocolate for use is simple and the results are rewarding. The melting instructions given here will be very detailed so that there will be no problem with the finished product.

Step 1
Some coatings come in wafers while others come in 10 lb. blocks or pieces broken from the block. If the candy is not already in small pieces, chip it into pieces no larger than ½ inch or 1.25 cm. in diameter.

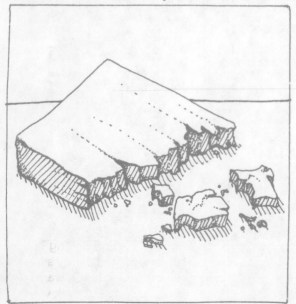

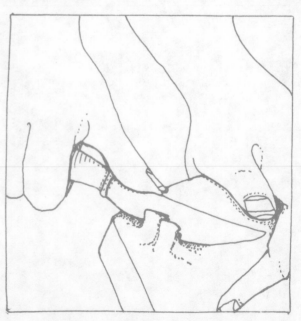

Step 2
Put the candy in a glass jar or pyrex bowl or dish. (I often use a pyrex pie plate.)

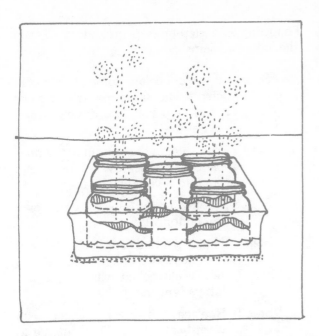

Step 3
Preheat oven to approximately 200° for five minutes. Then turn the oven temperature off. Note: NEVER leave candy in oven while heat is turned on. It will cause the candy to scorch.

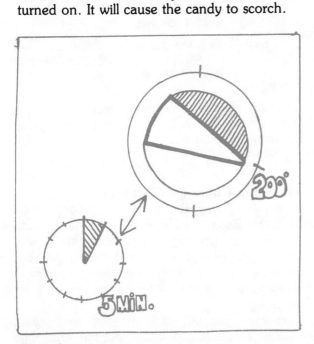

Step 4
Set candy, already chipped, in warm oven for twenty minutes.
Step 5
Check to see if candy is melted by trying to stir with a fork. (If candy isn't completely melted,

remove from oven and repeat steps 3 through 5.)

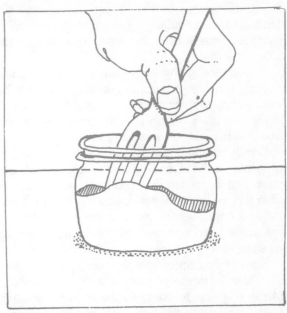

Step 6
When coating is thoroughly melted, remove from oven to a warm surface.

Using a Warming Surface
To keep candy coating from rehardening while working with it, the dish of melted candy should be placed on a warm surface, such as a warming tray, heating pad, or electric skillet. Check warm-

ing surface periodically to be sure it isn't getting too hot. If surface is too hot to touch, it is too hot for the candy. If this happens, lower the temperature by adjusting the thermostat or, if there is no thermostat, by pulling out the plug for a few minutes.

If you are going to use the melted candy coating quickly, a warming surface may not be necessary. However, if the candy rehardens while you are working with it, simply reheat the oven as instructed previously and remelt.

Candy coatings can be remelted any number of times without changing the quality of appearance or taste. If a piece of candy breaks after it is made, remelt it. If you need to melt additional candy of the same color, put candy in the same bowl and melt; the bowl need not be washed after each use.

Stir candy approximately every ten minutes. The heat from the warmer often causes the oils in the coatings to come to the top of the bowl, thus causing the finished candy to have streaks mixed through the chocolate.

Coloring Chocolate Coatings

Candy coatings should be colored with paste food colors. Do not attempt to use colorings with a water base. Paste colors are usually very concentrated. Therefore, after chocolate has been melted add only a small amount of coloring. I suggest the quantity of the size of a pea in a pound of chocolate. Stir and check color. If it is not dark enough, continue to add paste color in small amounts until desired shade is obtained.

Many times it is convenient to purchase white chocolate coating and be able to color it when necessary, thus eliminating the possibility of not having the right color candy needed for a certain recipe.

Tempering Chocolate

Tempering is a process of treating chocolate before molding to achieve shiny, perfect results. **Note: since coating chocolate has been pretreated before being purchased, it is not necessary to temper it.**

Pure milk chocolate **must** be tempered before being used. This is a somewhat difficult process which requires a very controlled temperature level of the chocolate at all times.

Following is a step-by-step procedure to help eliminate problems.

Step 1   If the chocolate comes in a block, chip it into small pieces and place in the top half of a double boiler. Set aside.

Step 2   Put water in the bottom of the double boiler, place over the fire, and bring to a vigorous boil.

Step 3   Put the top section of the pan over the bottom. Do not use a lid.

Step 4   Heat the chocolate to 105°F. Stir continuously until chocolate is nearly all melted with only a few lumps remaining.

Step 5   Replace the boiling water with warm water (125°F). Continue to stir until candy is completely melted.

Step 6   Again replace the water in the bottom pan with water of 65°F, and occasionally stir candy in top pan until it reaches 80°F.

Step 7   Replace the water again with that of 90°F. Stir chocolate until it reaches 86°F.

The chocolate is now ready for use, and this temperature should be maintained throughout the entire dipping process.

Flavoring Chocolate Coating

Highly concentrated oil based flavorings must be used to flavor candy coatings. They must, however, be used sparingly; start with ¼ teaspoon per pound of melted chocolate. Stir carefully and thoroughly, and taste. If a stronger flavor is desired, add a few drops more of the flavoring.

In most recipes, only the fondant, cream center is flavored, not the outside chocolate shell. Therefore, flavoring chocolate is not necessary.

Dietetic Coatings

Dietetic chocolate flavored coatings have a sugar

free base. They can be melted, flavored, and colored in the same ways described for regular coatings.

These coatings do not have the smooth chocolate taste of regular candy coatings. I recommend that you purchase only a small piece, taste it for your personal satisfaction, and then make a decision about getting a large quantity.

Diabetic Chocolate Coatings

The sweetener used in diabetic chocolate is usually manitol. Most diabetics can eat this type of candy. Check with your physician before using.

Carob Chocolate

This is a special type of chocolate for hyperactive individuals or those who favor health foods. This chocolate is somewhat expensive; it can be found in most health food stores.

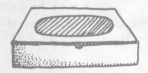

Molding Chocolate Flavored Coatings

Filling Molds

Spoon melted coating into cavity in clear plastic mold. Tap on table to remove air bubbles and refrigerate until set. When the bottom of the candy mold is cool, it is usually firm enough to remove. Turn mold upside down and flex gently. If candy does not release immediately, it has not been hardened sufficiently; return to refrigerator for a few minutes.

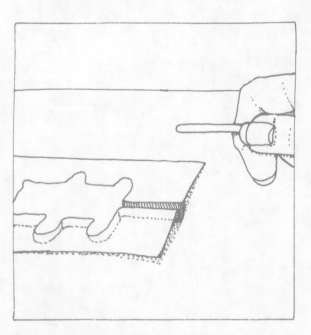

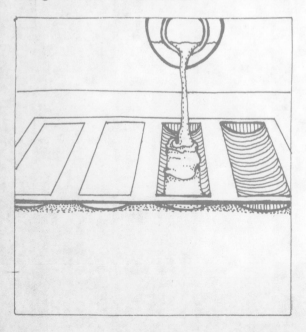

Candy Lollipops

The lollipops that I describe here are made of chocolate, not hard candy. Lollipop molds are made with a narrow cavity for the insertion of a sucker stick.

After the mold is filled as described in *Filling Molds*, insert the stick and give it two complete turns. Proceed with the directions for hardening.

Accenting or Painting a Mold

To achieve different colors on a piece of candy, the mold is painted before being filled. (The finished piece of candy is not painted with colored coating after it has been made.)

Dip a sucker stick or small brush into the desired color of melted chocolate. Paint the area you wish colored on the inside of the mold. Example: If you wish to make the inside of a rabbit's ear colored pink, dip your sucker stick into melted pink candy coating, and apply to that area on the inside of the rabbit mold.

Use a different stick for each color candy needed. If two colors touch, the one must be hardened in the refrigerator before applying the next color. All partially painted areas must be hardened before the mold is filled. The main color of the mold is usually left unpainted, for when the mold is filled with melted candy, all areas will be colored.

After selected areas have been painted and cooled, fill mold with melted candy coating, (insert sucker stick if making a lollipop,) tap mold on table to remove air bubbles and refrigerate until firm.

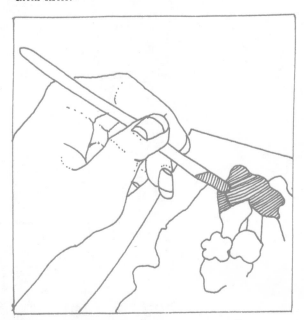

Hollow Molding

This type of molding can be done only with a two-piece mold which has a bottom. Fill the one section ¾ full. Carefully lay the counterpart on top and line up the buttons. Fasten together with tight clips. Turn mold slowly several times to in-sure candy reaching all areas. Tap on table to remove air bubbles. Refrigerate on one side for ten minutes; roll chocolate around inside again, refrigerate again until set on opposite side. Large molds may take half an hour to set.

Solid Molding

This is especially nice for solid Easter rabbits, crosses, and chicks. There are two methods for molding solid pieces, depending on the type of mold you have.

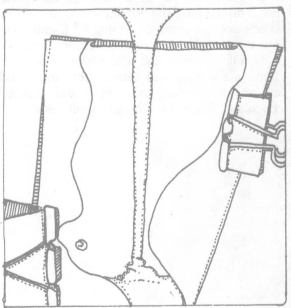

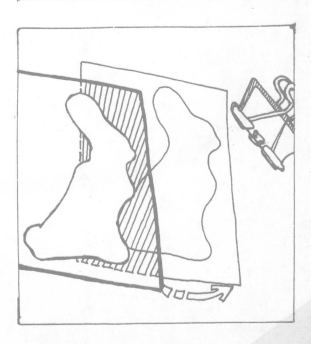

A. *Two-Piece Molds With The Bottom Cut Out.* (This is the one I prefer). These molds have alignment buttons; line up opposite sides and clip together with strong clips. If the clips are strong enough and several are used, the finished piece of candy will not need trimming. Fill the mold half full and tap on table to remove air bubbles. Finish filling to within ¼ inch from top, tap on table and refrigerate.

B. *Lay-On Method Of Solid Molding.* These molds do not have the bottom removed. Simply fill one section to within ¼ inch (1.25ml) from top, tap on table and refrigerate until firm. Set aside. Fill the other half with melted chocolate. Remove the hardened section from mold and lay on counterpart, now filled with melted chocolate. Place in refrigerator until chilled.

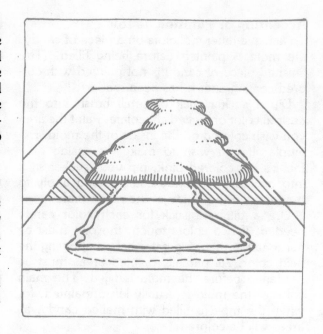

Holiday Specials

Halloween

As a special treat for halloweeners, small ghosts or candy pumpkins are a great idea. These are usually made into suckers and wrapped in small cellophane bags.

Thanksgiving

Traditional pumpkin pies are great; however, for a lighter dessert try filling a flat turkey mold with softened sherbet. Refrigerate until firm, let set at room temperature a few minutes, and unmold. Turn out on plates and return to freezer until ready to use.

Christmas

Gift wrap your homemade boxes of chocolate. The best gift to give a relative or friend is one with a personal touch. Your gift of confections will be gratefully appreciated. For a special professional touch, wrap a few pieces in small colored squares of foil. A good piece for this is a solid mint-flavored chocolate or one with a strawberry-flavored pink coating.

Candy Houses. A candy house mold has four cavities. Make two pieces of each of these sections, because the front of the house is also used as the back; the side is used twice; the roof section twice, etc.. After sections are made, place the front corner and one side section in place at right angles on a waxed, corrugated cardboard circle; pour melted chocolate down the inside corner and hold a few seconds until set. Do the sides of the house first, then the roof and last the chimney.

These houses can be filled with candy, peanuts, cookies, or any special treats before adding the roof.

Valentine's Day

Treat that special someone in your life with a valentine present of confection. Besides the traditional cardboard box, there is also now available a mold for making the box of chocolate and then filling it with creams and variety pieces as usual.

Easter

Filled Eggs. Molded or hand dipped eggs are a traditional Easter treat. The basic fondant is flavored for the various eggs. Traditional eggs include chocolate, coconut, fruit and nut, fudge, fudge-nut, cherry, cherry-coconut, cherry-nut, maple-nut, peanut butter, solid krispies, solid nut, and vanilla.

Half Egg Sections. A somewhat easier and faster filled egg can be made using only the top of the two piece egg mold. Coat the top section with melted chocolate flavored coating. Refrigerate until firm. Fill with cream center fondant and spoon melted chocolate on top. Tap on table to make smooth and refrigerate a few minutes to set.

Two-Piece Molds for Filled Easter Eggs. These are especially nice as filled Easter eggs. With a design on top, they look very professional and are easy to make.

To make a cream filled piece, coat both sections of the mold with melted chocolate coating. Refrigerate until set. Give a second thin coat of chocolate. If the chocolate doesn't run freely to sides when mold is turned, use a small brush to spread it around (I sometimes use my fingers). Refrigerate again until firm.

Fill both sections of mold with flavored fondant, (fruit & nut, maple-walnut, chocolate, whatever) until level. Spoon melted candy over edge (outside ridge) of both sections. Quickly turn one over the other, lining up buttons and clamp very tightly. Refrigerate until set.

Hollow Eggs with a Surprise Center. If one wishes to put a small surprise into the egg, simply make shell as suggested above and fill only the bottom half with jelly beans, mints, bubble gum, etc . . . Pour melted chocolate coating around outer edge of upper portion of mold, line up buttons, clamp, and refrigerate.

Here's a nice surprise for Grandmother! Make a hollow egg and seal a monetary gift in a clear plastic bag inside.

Marking Eggs. Immediately after removing egg from mold, place a candy flower or star on top to eliminate the confusion of not knowing what kind of egg you made.

If hand dipping eggs, simply place the flower on top of egg while chocolate is still soft. If you used a mold, place a small amount of warm chocolate on the bottom of the flower and set in place on egg after it has been completely made.

Hard candy flowers are available from candy supply houses; however they are not difficult to make. The recipe included in this book makes over 200 flowers or thousands of stars. These have a very long shelf life—several years. Since these are basically a sugar product, it is important that they are not exposed to excessive moisture. Although these are inexpensive to make, you may wish to purchase them if you plan to use only a few. The recipe for hard candy decorations can be found on page 24.

To mark candy eggs, choose a special color of flower to represent a specific kind of egg—a yellow flower could represent a peanut butter Easter egg. A color scheme chart has been included on page 23 for your convenience.

Solid Easter Pieces. No basket is complete without the traditional solid rabbits, hens, and

crosses. The rabbit molds are available in many sizes and shapes from 1 ounce to 1 pound.

For an elaborate looking piece of candy, paint the mold before filling. Carrots, flowers, eyes, ears, and paws or feet are often painted to accent a solid Easter piece. Refer to the section of how to paint mold (page 17) for more detailed instructions.

Baskets. The basket mold comes in two pieces. Clamp tightly and fill with chocolate. Refrigerate ten minutes and pour unset chocolate out of mold. Refrigerate basket again until firm. Remove clamps and carefully take basket from mold. Basket can then be filled with marzipan strawberries, a variety of piece candies; or after adding a little Easter grass, fill with small Easter pieces, that is, rabbits, hens, eggs, and jelly beans. This basket also is a great idea for a birthday present.

Easter Huts (Panorama Eggs). This is a hollow egg with an opening in front. A scene is then placed inside the egg.

A special mold is made for the panorama egg. It appears as an oval shaped, smooth egg with an opening in the front. It comes in two sections and should be clamped tightly before using. Fill approximately half full with melted chocolate and roll to coat the inside of the shell. Pour out excess chocolate. Refrigerate mold until firm. Repeat this procedure—it gives the egg a solid coat of chocolate. (I especially like this done in a pastel color coating chocolate.)

Secure candy or plastic bunnies, crosses, or flowers in opening with a small amount of melted chocolate. Decorate opening to cavity and top of egg with hard candy icing flowers and stars.

Weddings

Wedding Mints. One of the best mints for a wedding or dinner party would be Wendy's Wedding Mints (page 38). It is not only easy to make, but has a taste such as that of the finest confection shops. These mints can be made several days before the wedding for they keep well if stored in an air tight container.

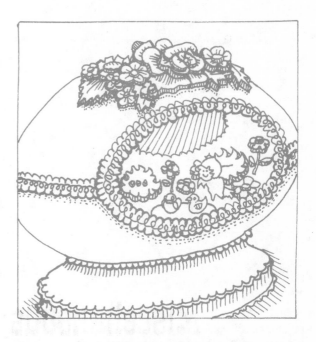

Ice. Don't forget to freeze water in a large heart shaped mold for use in the punch.

Graduation

Chocolate is often molded in small shapes representing graduation symbols for party treats.

Miscellaneous but Important

Marking Candy Pieces

There are several ways to mark candy with cream centers so you can identify each piece without a problem. (Thus, it is no longer necessary to bite into a piece of candy to tell what type of center was used.)

Any of the following methods will identify your candy varieties.

Method A. Mark each piece of candy with a particular center; use a certain color candy flower. Example: place a small candy decoration on the top of each finished piece. A yellow flower is often placed on a peanut butter or lemon cream. Thus you can easily recognize all such creams by the yellow decoration on top.

Method B. Use different colored chocolate to make the outer shell. If using only the cordial mold for making all the different creams, use a green colored coating for shells of peppermint creams, pink coating for raspberry creams, orange coating for orange creams, etc. Using this method, only one mold is needed for making a variety box of candy.

Method C. Make creams in a small mold or hand dip. Fill a ketchup squeeze bottle with warm candy and write letter on top of each piece after it has been made and cooled. Example: put the letter C on all chocolate creams, L on lemon creams, M on maple creams, etc. To keep chocolate melted in squeeze bottle between uses, carefully set in pan of warm water after each use.

Coloring Coconut

Put 1 cup flake coconut in a jar with a few drops liquid food coloring. After placing on lid, shake vigorously.

Coloring Sugar

Place sugar in a jar, add a few drops of liquid food coloring and shake until evenly colored. Spread out on cookie sheet to dry. Store in an air tight container.

Toasting Coconut

Put angel flake or macaroon coconut in pie pan and place in oven which has been preheated to 375°F. Stir often to brown evenly. Remove from oven when sufficiently browned.

Problems and Remedies

Chocolate coating overheated. If chocolate

coating has been slightly overheated, it will become stiff and difficult to use. Add a few para-mont crystals or 1 teaspoon of solid vegetable shortening per pound of chocolate coating. Often this softens the chocolate enough for use. If it is still stiff, do not attempt to use. Coating will not become overheated as long as it is not placed in the oven under direct heat. However it will scorch if exposed to temperature above 225°F.

Chocolate appears stiff (not from overheating). If chocolate has been exposed to high humidity, it may become stiff and not tend to melt smoothly. After melting add a few drops paramont crystals or one teaspoon of solid vegetable shortening per pound of chocolate flavored coating.

The coatings have a shelf life of over a year provided they are not exposed to high humidity. To preserve candy coatings over a long period of time, I recommend freezing them; however the quality may change slightly. Freeze only the

Color Scheme Chart

Color	Fondant Flavor for Creams	Easter Egg Centers	Flower Color Used on Top of Eggs	Hard Candy
WHITE	Peppermint Vanilla	Vanilla cream Coconut	Vanilla cream Coconut	Wintergreen
PINK	Strawberry Raspberry Cherry	Cherry Cherry coconut Cherry-nut	Cherry Cherry coconut Cherry-nut	
GREEN	Lime	Pistachio	Pistachio	Spearmint
RED				Cinnamon
YELLOW	Butter cream Banana Lemon Pineapple Peanut butter	Peanut butter	Peanut butter	Banana cream Pineapple
BLACK				Anise Licorice
ORANGE	Orange	Fruit & Nut	Fruit & Nut	
PURPLE	Grape			
BROWN	Fudge Chocolate	Fudge Chocolate cream Solid nut Solid krispie		Root beer
BLUE			Fudge Fudge-nut Chocolate Solid nut Solid krispie	
BEIGE	Maple cream	Maple-nut	Maple-nut	Sassafras

coating. Do not attempt to make the candy and then freeze it.

Chocolate coating not available in your area. If candy coatings are not available in your area, they may be ordered from a retail outlet. Care should be taken not to order candy coatings if the weather is too warm. These coatings have a low melting point.

A satisfactory substitute for chocolate coating can be made by melting 12 ounces chocolate chips (either semi-sweet or milk chocolate) and ¼ block paraffin (which has been chipped) in the top of a double boiler. Use low heat and stir continuously until melted.

If pure milk chocolate is available, it also can be made into a coating chocolate by adding paraffin. Use ¼ block of chipped paraffin per pound of chocolate and follow melting instructions for chocolate chip coating. When paraffin is added to pure milk chocolate, it is not necessary to temper it.

Selection of Molds

Only a few molds are very important for the making of professional type candy. The two basic molds are the *cordial mold* and the

holding tray.

The *cordial mold* is used to make chocolate-covered cherries, creams, and bon-bons.

The *holding tray* is a mold with several low cavities which hold the small fluted paper cups. When making nut clusters, haystacks, or any drop pieces of candy, the cups are held in place with this tray. Candy is dropped into the cups and then placed in the refrigerator to harden. Peanut butter cups and mallow cups also utilize the holding tray.

If a holding tray is not available in your area, substitute the peanut butter cup mold for it. It is a mold already having the fluted ridges on the side. The piece of candy then has fluted edges but, when placed in the paper cup, doesn't adhere to the paper.

The two basic molds are the only ones needed to make a variety box of candy. However, caramels and nougets are nice when molded in small square shapes.

Seasonal and all-occasion molds are available for holidays and special events. Use your own discretion as to which ones you select. The smaller ones are usually favored by mothers and children.

Hard Candy Decorations

2	**large egg whites**
1	**pound confectioners sugar**
¼	**teaspoon cream of tartar**

Bring eggs to room temperature by holding under warm running water. Combine egg whites with confectioners sugar and cream of tartar in large bowl; beat at highest speed until thick—approximately ten minutes. Cover bowl with damp cloth to prevent drying and becoming hard while working.

Star Flower Decorations. *For sugar cube and candy decorations.* Color a small amount of icing desired shade. Using a decorating syringe or bag, press star shaped decorations onto a sheet of wax paper. Set aside to air dry overnight. When hardened, carefully remove from wax paper.

Birthday Cake Decorations. *Similar to the ones you buy at the party supply counter of a grocery store.* Select a large picture with very little detail from a coloring book. Lay this page on the table and tape a sheet of wax paper on top. Color candy icing desired colors. Using a star tube, "star" in all areas of the picture. Be sure to keep stars close together forming a solid figure. Set aside to air dry overnight. (Mother Goose characters are especially nice to do.) Peel from paper when completely dry.

These decorations will keep for months if kept in an air tight container after being hardened.

Miscellanea

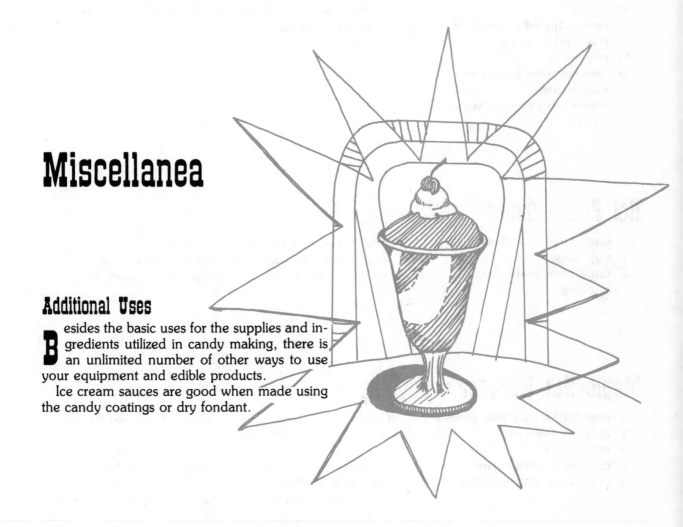

Additional Uses

Besides the basic uses for the supplies and ingredients utilized in candy making, there is an unlimited number of other ways to use your equipment and edible products.

Ice cream sauces are good when made using the candy coatings or dry fondant.

Butter Pecan Ice Cream Topping

1 cup dark corn syrup
1 cup dry fondant
½ cup water
1 cup pecan halves
¼ teaspoon butter flavoring

Combine dry fondant and water in sauce pan and boil 5 minutes.

Add corn syrup and continue heating until mixture starts to boil. Remove from heat and add flavoring. Pour over pecan halves.

French Mint Ice Cream Sauce

2 cups sugar
2 tablespoons light corn syrup
1 cup chipped chocolate flavored coating
¾ cup milk
3 tablespoons butter or margarine
½ teaspoon peppermint extract

Combine sugar, corn syrup, chocolate coating, and milk. Stir over medium heat until mixture boils. Continue cooking for 2 minutes. Remove from heat and add butter and peppermint extract.

Hot Fudge Sauce

12 ounces evaporated milk
1 cup sugar
2 cups chocolate flavored coating

Heat ingredients together in saucepan.
When chocolate melts, beat until mixture boils and slightly thickens. Can be stored in refrigerator for later use.

Maple-Nut Ice Cream Topping

1 cup broken walnut pieces
1 cup dry fondant
¼ cup water
1 cup light corn syrup
¼ teaspoon maple extract

Cover walnuts with water in saucepan and boil 2 minutes. Drain water and set nuts aside.
Combine dry fondant and water in saucepan. Boil 5 minutes. Add corn syrup and maple extract. Stir and pour over walnuts. Store in jar in refrigerator for later use.
Note: Sugar can be substituted for dry fondant in this recipe.

Hot Caramel Ice Cream Sauce

1 cup caramelized sweetened condensed milk*
⅓ cup evaporated milk
2 tablespoons sugar

Heat above ingredients in heavy saucepan over low heat until mixture becomes smooth and starts to boil. Continue to cook for two minutes. Serve hot or cold over ice cream.
*To caramelize the sweetened condensed milk, refer to Easy Soft Caramels (page 66).

Marshmallow Ice Cream Topping

2 tablespoons water
½ cup dry fondant
1 cup marshmallow cream

Combine water and dry fondant in saucepan. Place over low heat until mixture starts to boil. Remove from heat; stir in marshmallow cream until smooth.
Note: Granulated sugar can be substituted for dry fondant; however, water should be increased to ¼ cup.

Decorating Cakes

Even an amateur baker can decorate cakes to have a professional appearance when using molded candy. Select molds that are appropriate for that particular occasion. "Paint" the molds before filling with colored or dark chocolate. Set in refrigerator until hardened.

Frost cake and lay candy decoration in place. Put a border of small icing stars around the candy to secure it in place.

A cake decorated for Halloween becomes somewhat creepy when a candy witch is surrounded by bats and spiders.

Holiday scenes can be easily shown on such a cake. Frost the top half of the cake in a light blue colored icing to represent the sky, and the bottom half in green colored icing, representing the grass or field. Sprinkle green colored coconut over the grass area. Arrange candy shapes on cake. Pilgrims might be hunting turkeys or children could be playing in the grass on such a cake.

Additional Uses of Molds

Hard Candy Pieces

Although the clear plastic molds are designed for the purpose of melted candy coatings, they can also be used for hard candy suckers. Follow recipe for Hard Candy (page 64). After candy reaches the required cooking temperature, remove from heat and stir for 3 minutes to cool slightly. Spoon candy into molds and insert sucker stick. Do not attempt to pour candy from pan into mold because it will cause the mold to bend.

Plaster Crafts

Purchase plaster for crafts from a hardware or craft store. Follow instructions for mixing which are given on the box. Pour into mold and let set until dry; it will then release easily. Painting "plaques" can be done with any type of water or oil colors. I recommend the use of magic markers. If finished product will be hung on the wall, insert a paper clip in back of mold immediately after pouring plaster.

Molding Ice Creams and Sherbets

Softened ice cream and sherbet can be molded. Fill molds and place in freezer until very solid. To unmold, turn upside down on plate. Let set at room temperature a few minutes and place a warm cloth on top. This can be done only with large molds with very few details. Decorations can be added using a standard cake decorator and creamy frosting.

This is especially nice when used as ice cream bells for a wedding, green sherbet trees for Christmas or chocolate ice cream footballs for your son's birthday.

Molded Ice

Fill molds with water, place in freezer for that special ice shape. Pre-chilled punch takes on an added touch when the ice floating on top has been molded.

Fondue Dip

Fresh fruits are especially good when dipped in melted chocolate. Clean and slice fresh fruits and insert toothpicks. Place melted chocolate flavored coating in fondue pot and dip fruit.

Recipes for Professional Type Candy

Clusters

Clusters are made by mixing a snack with melted white or chocolate flavored coating. The number of different kinds of clusters you can make is limited only by one's imagination. Given for you are the basic clusters found in a variety box of confections.

Nut Clusters

1½ cups nuts or chopped nuts (Cashews, Pecans, Peanuts, Walnuts)
1 pound melted coating chocolate

Mix nuts with melted chocolate.
Fill into fluted paper cups being held in a holding tray, or drop by spoonfulls onto a lightly greased baking sheet. Place in refrigerator until hard.

Raisin Clusters

1 cup dark raisins
2 cups melted chocolate coating

Combine above ingredients and drop by spoonfuls onto a greased cookie sheet. Refrigerate until firm.

Peanut Butter Peanut Clusters I

½   cup smooth peanut but-
     ter
1   cup peanuts
2   cups coating chocolate

Add peanut butter and peanuts to melted chocolate. Place fluted paper cups in holding tray. Fill ¾ full with candy mixture and place in freezer until hard.

Peanut Butter Peanut Clusters II

1   cup peanuts
2   cups melted peanut but-
     ter
     candy coating

Mix coating and peanuts together. Drop by spoonfuls onto a lightly oiled cookie sheet or waxed paper. Put in freezer to set.

Rocky Road Candy

½   cup miniture marsh-
     mallows
½   cup chopped walnuts
12   ounces melted
     chocolate coating

Add marshmallows and walnuts to chocolate and stir. Drop from a teaspoon onto a greased baking sheet. Place in freezer until set.

Crispie Clusters

1   cup crispied rice cereal
1   cup melted chocolate
     flavored coating

Add cereal to melted candy coating and stir. Spoon into fluted paper cups which have been placed in a holding tray. Refrigerate until hardened.

Chocolate Haystacks—Coconut Clusters

1   cup fine macaroon
     coconut
2   cups melted chocolate
     coating

Add coconut to melted candy coating. Spoon into peanut butter cup mold or drop by spoonfuls onto waxed paper. Refrigerate until solid.

Creamy White Haystacks

1 **cup fine macaroon coconut**
2 **cups melted white coating**

Mix coating and coconut together. Drop from teaspoon onto waxed paper to cool and harden, in refrigerator if necessary.

Cordials, Creams, and Bonbons

Outer Shells

The chocolate covered cherry mold is used for cordials, creams, and bonbons.

After melting the chocolate as previously directed, spoon a small amount of candy coating into each cavity. Using a sucker stick, brush, or your finger, coat the sides on the cavity. Refrigerate until it is hardened. To check to see if your chocolate layer is thick enough, hold mold up to light, if there are any thin spots, recoat only that area and let harden. This completes the outside shell.

Now, for the centers, follow directions for cordials, creams and bonbons.

Cordials

Canned fruit or candied fruit may be used for cordials. The best known type of cordial is the chocolate covered cherry. For excellent results, I recommend using maraschino cherries. Follow previous directions for coating mold cavities with chocolate flavored coating. Place cherry in hardened candy cavity and set aside. In a small dish, mix ½ cup dry fondant with 2 tablespoons cherry juice or water. Spoon this mixture around cherry in cavity to within ⅛ inch from top of cavity. Now, starting around the outside edge, spoon melted chocolate over top. Tap mold on table and refrigerate until firm. Remove from mold. Let set 24 hours before serving. The acid in the cherry causes the dry fondant mixture to liquefy.

When making cherries, a thicker dry fondant mixture may be desired; use only 1½ tablespoons liquid with fondant. The chocolate bottom is then easier to put on. However, it will take several days for the center to become completely liquefied. If you wish to use more fruit juice than the specified amount the center will liquefy in several hours.

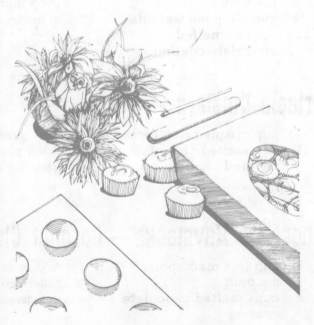

Green Mint Cherries

Follow the basic directions for making chocolate covered cherries but substitute green maraschino cherries for the red ones. Mix 1 drop oil of peppermint with the fondant mixture before filling the candy shells. Continue as directed.

Liquor Cherries

Marinate cherries to be used for cordials in any type of whiskey or brandy for at least three days (I recommend the use of rum for liquor cherries.) Using this as the liquid, make the fondant mixture as directed under cordials as for chocolate covered cherries. Continue as directed under that section.

Fruit Cordials

Besides the traditional cherry cordial, try these other canned fruit varieties: pineapple, grape, and peach. If the piece of fruit is too large for the chocolate candy shell, simply cut in half.

Creams

The outer shells for creams are made the same as **cordials.** Follow directions carefully. After shell is removed from refrigerator, a cream fondant center may be spooned into the cavity. The creams we refer to here are made with either creamy white fondant or dry fondant. Creamy white fondant is a basic, white, unflavored cream center. Dry fondant resembles powdered sugar and must have water added to it when being used for creams. A cream made with dry fondant is somewhat sweeter and smoother than a creamy white fondant. Dry fondant creams must ripen or be left set at room temperature for 12 hours before using.

Peppermint Cream I

1   cup creamy white fondant
3   drops peppermint oil
    Green candy coating for outer shells

Mix fondant and peppermint oil thoroughly. Follow directions for making **Creams.**

Peppermint Creams II

1   tablespoon light corn syrup
½   cup dry fondant
2   tablespoons water
2   drops peppermint oil
    Green coating for shell

Combine above ingredients, except green coating, in a small dish. Follow directions as specified under **Creams.**

Coconut Cream

1 cup creamy white fondant
½ cup fine macaroon coconut
¼ cup marshmallow cream
Chocolate flavored coating for shells

Mix fondant, coconut, and marshmallow cream until well blended. Using melted chocolate, make outer shells, harden in refrigerator and follow the instructions for filling as directed under **Creams.**

Raspberry Creams

1 cup creamy white fondant
3 drops oil of raspberry
Pink candy coating for shell

Using the cordial mold, make outer shell of pink candy coating. If creamy white fondant is a little stiff, knead to make smooth. Mix flavoring with fondant. Fill hardened candy shell with fondant. Put melted candy coating on top to seal and refrigerate until firm.

Maple Creams

1 cup creamy white fondant
¼ teaspoon maple extract or mapleline
Butterscotch or chocolate candy coating for shell

Cream fondant and extract together. Spoon into butterscotch or chocolate shell.
Note: Chopped walnuts may be added to the above recipe to make maple-walnut centers.

Cherry Creams

1 cup creamy white fondant
4 drops cherry flavored oil
¼ cup candied cherries
Chocolate coating for shell

Cut cherries into fine pieces. Mix fondant, oil, and candied cherries together. Using cordial mold, make outer shell of melted chocolate and refrigerate. When shell is hardened, fill with cherry cream mixture. Spoon melted chocolate coating on top and again refrigerate until firm.

Lemon Creams

1 cup creamy white fondant
3 drops lemon oil
1 teaspoon grated lemon rind
Yellow candy coating for shell

Make candy shells from yellow candy coating (follow directions under **Cordials** page 30).   Blend until smooth: fondant, oil, and lemon rind. Spoon cream center into shells. Cover top with melted coating and refrigerate to cool.

French Vanilla Cream

1 cup creamy white fon-
dant
1 cup melted white
coating

Combine fondant and candy coating. Work with a spatula until thoroughly mixed. Use as cream center for any small mold.

Chocolate Fudge Cream

1 cup semi-sweet coating
½ cup sweetened, con-
densed milk
Chocolate or white
coating for shells

Preheat oven to 200°F, then turn off. Place 1 cup semi-sweet coating in oven for 20 minutes, remove from oven and stir. Add sweetened, condensed milk and stir until thoroughly blended. This is a rich dark cream center.

Follow directions for **Cordials** (page 30) for making the outer shell.

Vanilla Creams

1 cup creamy white fon-
dant
4 drops white vanilla
flavoring
1 drop almond flavoring

Combine fondant, white vanilla flavoring, and almond flavoring. Blend thoroughly.

Buttercreams I

Follow directions for buttercream frosting mix. This makes a good tasting confection. However, dut to the butter content, it should be consumed within a few days.

Buttercreams II

2 pounds confectioners
sugar
½ pound butter
1 cup marshmallow cream

Mix above ingredients until well blended. Kneed until smooth.

Chocolate Rum Truffles

½	cup dry fondant
2	tablespoons rum
½	ounce liquid unsweetened baking chocolate
⅓	cup finely chopped walnuts

Mix dry fondant and rum in small dish; stir in unsweetened chocolate and walnuts.

Sloe Berries

2	tablespoons sloe gin
½	cup dry fondant

Combine above ingredients in a small dish and mix well.

Butter Rum Squares

2	tablespoons rum
½	cup dry fondant
1	teaspoon softened butter

Mix above ingredients in bowl until well blended. The small square mold is nice for this recipe. (Due to the butter, this confection can be kept only a few days.)

Amaretto Surprise

1½	tablespoons amaretto liqueur
½	cup dry fondant
	whole almonds

Mix liqueur and dry fondant in bowl until well blended. Place whole almond in hardened candy shell and spoon fondant mixture around nut.

Whiskey Cherries

Refer to section on **Liquor Cherries** (page 31).

Piña Coladas

¼	cup piña colada
¾	cup dry fondant
¼	cup dry, fine coconut
1	tablespoon vodka

Mix ingredients together in small dish.

Grapevine Creams

2 tablespoons sweet grape wine
½ cup dry fondant

Combine above ingredients in small dish and stir until smooth.

Creamed Mints

5 tablespoons crème de menthe
1 cup dry fondant
  Melted green coating chocolate

Stir crème de menthe and dry fondant together in small dish until well blended. Use green coating when making outer shell for these mint-flavored creams.

Chocolate Drops

3 tablespoons cold water
1 egg white
1 pound confectioners sugar
¼ teaspoon white vanilla

Blend water, egg white, and vanilla with a fork. Add confectioners sugar until mixture becomes as thick as paste. Additional confectioners sugar may be required.

Using the cordial mold, make outer shell of chocolate. Follow further directions under **Cordial** section (page 30).

Bonbons

The outer shell of bonbons in this section is made with candy coating using the same procedure as outlined for **Cordials** (page 30). For the hard sugar shells used on bonbons, refer to "Bonbon Glaze" (page 75).

Any pastel-colored coating makes a nice shell for bonbons. After making shells, use one of the following recipes.

Bonbons I

2 pounds confectioners sugar
1 can sweetened, condensed milk (15 ounces)
1 pound coconut
½ cup margarine, melted and cooled

Mix together and knead. Make into balls and put in refrigerator to chill for 1 hour. Use as a filling for bonbon centers.

Bonbons II

¾ **cup light corn syrup**
2 **cups fine macaroon coconut**

Heat corn syrup until it starts to boil. Pour over coconut and stir. Cover and let set 1 hour before using as a center for bonbons.

Bonbons III

2 **cups fine macaroon coconut**
¾ **cup light corn syrup**
½ **cup marshmallow cream**

Cook corn syrup and marshmallow cream just until boiling. Remove from heat and pour over macaroon coconut. Stir; let set 1 hour before using.

Mints

Mints are usually made from green or chocolate flavored coating. To prepare the candy coating for use, preheat the oven to 200°F and turn off. Place dish of candy pieces in oven for approximately 20 minutes. Remove from heat and stir. (For more detailed instructions, refer to section for preparing the candy coating (page 12).

Peppermint Patties I

8 **ounces melted green coating**
1 **pound cream white fondant**
Few drops peppermint oil

Coat sides of patty mold with melted coating and refrigerate until firm. Add peppermint flavoring to fondant and stir thoroughly. When candy hardens in mold, remove from refrigerator. Spoon fondant into mold to within ⅛ inch of the top. Cover top of mold with melted coating, being sure to seal all sides. Tap on table until smooth and place in refrigerator until set.

Peppermint Patties II

8 **ounces melted chocolate flavored coating**
½ **cup dry fondant**
2 **tablespoons water**
2 **drops peppermint oil**

Coat sides of patty mold with a thin layer of chocolate coating. Place in refrigerator. Add water and peppermint oil to dry fondant and stir until well blended (for a thinner fondant, add more water). When candy in peppermint patty mold hardens, remove from cooling area. Spoon fondant mixture into candy lined mold to within ⅛ inch of the opening. Place a spoon of melted chocolate over top to seal.

Tap on table and place in refrigerator until firm.

Cream Cheese Mints

1 small package cream cheese (3 ounces)
1 pound confectioners sugar
3 drops peppermint oil

Soften cream cheese with fork, add peppermint oil and stir vigorously. Add confectioners sugar until stiff enough to form small balls.

Dip rubber molds into sugar. Press candy into mold using palm of hand. Turn out on waxed paper.

(Since this recipe uses dairy products, I recommend that they be consumed within a few days.)

Butter Mints

½ cup softened butter
2 pounds confectioners sugar
¼ cup whipping cream (do not whip)
5 drops peppermint oil *

Combine butter, whipping cream, oil flavoring and half of the confectioners sugar in a large bowl. Slowly stir in just enough remaining sugar so that stiff balls can be formed. Dip a rubber mold into sugar and press in candy. Turn out onto waxed paper.

Fresh mints will be softer and taste better than those that were made several days ahead of consumption. Do not attempt to keep mints more than a few days.

* ½ teaspoon peppermint extract can be substituted for the oil.

French Mints

8 ounces melted chocolate flavored coating
4 ounces melted green coating
3 drops peppermint oil

Flavor green coating with peppermint oil and set aside. Using a mold having small square cavities, put a spoon of melted chocolate in each cavity so that it is ⅓ full. Set in refrigerator until it just starts to get hard.

Next, add a layer of flavored green candy and return to the cooling area until slightly hardened. Now finish filling the cavity with melted chocolate. Return to refrigerator until solid.

Bavarian Mints

16 ounces melted chocolate coating
5 drops peppermint oil

Separate melted chocolate into 2 dishes; one approximately 10 ounces and the other 6 ounces. Add peppermint flavoring to the 6 ounce dish of chocolate. Using a mold with small square shapes, coat mold with chocolate and fill the cavity half full. Refrigerate until solid. Now, add the peppermint flavored chocolate until the cavity is full. Place in refrigerator until it is hardened.

Peppermint Swirl

8　ounces melted white coating
8　ounces melted pink coating
4　drops peppermint oil

Mix peppermint flavoring with pink coating. Lightly oil a cookie sheet. Pour melted pink coating on the cookie sheet in four piles. Pour melted white coating over and around pink. With a spoon, mix the candy slightly, just until it becomes swirled.

Wendy's Wedding Mints

16　ounces melted white candy coating
6　drops peppermint oil
　　Hard candy flowers

Mix flavoring and white coating. After placing fluted paper cups in holding tray, spoon candy coating into paper cups until ¾ full. Center a small candy flower on top of each piece. Refrigerate candy, still in holding tray, until firm.

If a holding tray is not available in your area, substitute a peanut butter cup mold.

Peppermint Crowns

16　ounces melted chocolate flavored coating
¼　teaspoon peppermint oil
*1　package sandwich cookies

Combine the oil flavoring and melted candy. Using ice tongs, dip a cookie into the melted dish of candy, shake off excess and lay on a lightly oiled cookie sheet. Place in refrigerator unitl hardened.

*For best results, select the cookies that are dark wafers with a white cream icing center.

Drop Mints

1　cup cream white fondant
4　drops peppermint oil
　　Few drops liquid food color

Place fondant in double boiler, add oil flavoring and food coloring. Heat just until melted. Turn off heat and remove from double boiler. Drop by teaspoonfulls onto a ribbed rubber-mat. Peel off when cool.

These mints are very attractive in pastel colors of pink, green, white, or yellow.

If candy becomes too thick to make smooth mints, place top candy pan back over hot water from double boiler until fondant becomes soft.

Caramels

Caramels are always a welcome treat. Sometimes a soft caramel is needed for certain candy varieties, such as turtles or a piece of candy with a soft caramel center. Most recipes require caramel cooking temperatures of 248°F for a firm, cut piece of candy. This kind would be cut into squares, dipped in chocolate coating, or wrapped in waxed paper.

Most recipes can be adapted for use of a soft caramel by simply not cooking as long. Cook only to 235°F for a soft caramel.

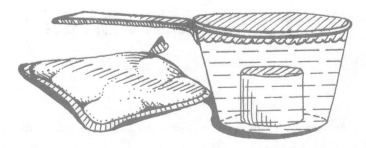

Brown Sugar Caramels

2	cups brown sugar
1	cup molasses
½	cup semi-sweet coating chocolate
¼	cup margarine
1	cup milk
1	cup chopped nuts

In a heavy saucepan combine sugar, molasses, chocolate, margarine and milk. Cook for approximately 20 minutes over low heat (246°F). Pour onto a buttered cookie sheet. Cut when nearly cold. These can then be dipped in coating chocolate and wrapped individually in waxed paper.

If using this caramel as a center for a filled piece of candy, coat cordial or small square mold with candy coating, let harden, and fill with caramel which has been cooked to only 235°F.

Easy Soft Caramels

1	can sweetened, condensed milk

Remove paper label and completely immerse unopened can of milk in a pan of water. Place over medium heat until water boils. Lower heat until water temperature is maintained just at boiling point. Continue to cook for five hours. Add boiling water as needed to keep the unopened can completely covered with water at all times. After required cooking time has elapsed, remove pan of water from heat. Cool canned milk in the cooking water until the water reaches room temperature. Milk, which has now caramelized, is ready for use.

Note: Several cans of milk can be prepared at a time.

Traditional Caramels

15	ounces sweetened, condensed milk
8	ounces dark corn syrup
½	cup butter or margarine
1	pound brown sugar

Combine all ingredients. Keep stirring over heat until mixture begins to boil, lower heat and continue boiling until it forms a hard ball, approximately 245°F. For a softer caramel, heat to only 235°F.

Traditional Candy Bars and Pieces

Fluff

This is an airy, soft center for a piece of candy. It is very good when used in the small candy bar mold.

½	cup marshmallow cream
8	ounces melted candy coating

Beat marshmallow cream and melted coating until well blended. Any of the following coatings are suggested: peanut butter, white, chocolate, or butterscotch.

Caramel Fluff Bar

Coat small candy bar mold with melted chocolate, and refrigerate until firm. Spoon in a thin layer of soft brown sugar caramels. To this, add a layer of white coating Fluff. Cover bottom of mold with melted chocolate. Tap on table to make smooth and refrigerate.

Pecan-Raisin Bark

½	cup raisins
¾	cup broken pecan pieces
1	pound melted chocolate flavored coating

Mix ingredients and pour onto a lightly oiled baking sheet to a depth of ½ inch. Refrigerate only until firm enough to touch so that it doesn't stick to your fingers. Score and cut into 1 inch squares. Return to refrigerator until hardened.

Scotch Almond Bark

4	ounces slivered almonds
1	pound melted butterscotch coating

Mix almonds and butterscotch coating together. Pour in a thin layer ¼ inch on a lightly oiled baking sheet. Rub with a spoon when it starts to get firm. This forms a bark texture. Place in refrigerator until hardened. Break apart with hands.

Chocolate Bark

4 ounces cashews
1 pound coating chocolate

Combine nuts and melted chocolate flavored coating. Pour candy onto a lightly greased cookie sheet to a depth of ¼ inch. Form a rough bark texture by rubbing a spoon across the top. Refrigerate until set. Break apart with hands.

Peanut Butter Royal

½ cup smooth peanut butter
1 pound melted candy coating

Mix peanut butter with white or chocolate candy coating. Stir until thoroughly blended. Pour onto a lightly greased sheet to a depth of ½ inch.

Butterscotch Susans

1 pound melted butterscotch coating
½ cup crunchy peanut butter
Round snack crackers

Break crackers in half, or cut it with a sharp knife. Combine candy coating and crunchy peanut butter; stir until blended. Using ice tongs, dip cracker pieces into mixture and lay on lightly greased cookie sheet. Place in refrigerator or freezer until hardened.

Dipped Caramels

Caramels may be purchased or made; however, it usually costs as much to make them as to buy them.

Place caramel on a fork (dipping fork or table fork) and dip into melted chocolate coating. Rub bottom of fork along edge of dish to remove excess chocolate. Turn upside down on lightly greased baking sheet or waxed paper. Place in refrigerator until firm.

Chocolate Covered Pretzels

Knotted pretzels have the best success for dipping. Hold pretzel with ice tongs and dip into melted white or chocolate coating. Pretzels can be either salted or unsalted.

Shake slightly to remove excess chocolate. Place on greased cookie sheet and refrigerate.

Turtles

Pecan or walnut halves
Soft caramel recipe
Melted coating
chocolate

Drop a teaspoon of melted chocolate on a lightly oiled baking sheet. (Twelve pieces of candy can be made simultaneously on a 9" x 12" sheet.) Tap briskly on table to make chocolate smooth into a thin layer. Lay nuts on chocolate. Refrigerate until firm. Spoon on caramel and quickly cover with melted chocolate. Be sure to cover all of caramel and seal with bottom chocolate.

Almond Coconut Bars

¼ cup light corn syrup
½ cup fine macaroon
coconut
Almonds
Coating chocolate

Heat corn syrup until very hot but not boiling. Pour over coconut and mix well. Set aside for 30 minutes.

Coat small candy bar mold with melted chocolate and refrigerate. When hardened, lay three or four almonds in bottom and fill with coconut mixture. Spoon on melted chocolate to seal. Place in refrigerator.

Toffee Bars I

1¾ cup sugar
1 pound butter
½ cup light corn syrup
Chopped walnuts
Coating cocolate for
dipping

Cook above ingredients to 300°F. Pour onto a baking sheet to depth of ¼ inch. Sprinkle with nuts. Score and cut as soon as possible. When cold, dip into melted coating chocolate and refrigerate.

Toffee Bars II

¼ cup margarine
¼ cup butter
1 cup brown sugar
Chopped walnuts
Melted coating
chocolate for dipping

In a heavy saucepan, melt margarine and butter over low heat. Add brown sugar. Bring to a boil and cook slowly to 300°F. Stir constantly to prevent candy from sticking. Pour onto a cookie sheet and sprinkle with nuts. When candy starts to cool, score with a sharp knife. Break apart pieces when cold and dip in melted coating chocolate.

Note: When making Toffee bars do not substitute margarine for butter.

Heavenly Hash

½ cup flaked coconut
1 cup creamy white fon-
dant
8 ounces melted white
coating chocolate

Soften fondant by kneading in a glass baking dish. Add melted white coating and work with spatula until well blended. Knead in coconut. Roll mixture into small balls and dip into melted pastel colored candy coating. Place on waxed paper and set in freezer just until hard. These are best when eaten the same day.

Peanut Butter Cups

Peanut butter cups can be made in either the peanut butter cup mold or holding tray.

Using the fluted edge mold—spoon melted chocolate flavored coating into mold until mold is approximately ¼ full. Using finger or small brush, coat bottom and sides evenly. Refrigerate until firm. Spoon peanut butter cream recipe into center of hardened candy cup to ¼ inch from top. Cover with melted chocolate and place in refrigerator until firm.

Using a holding tray—place fluted paper cups in holding tray. Spoon 1 teaspoon melted chocolate coating into cups and spread evenly to bottom and edges. This can be done efficiently and quickly by using your index finger. Set tray with candy coated cups in refrigerator to harden. Fill with your favorite peanut butter cream center recipe. Spoon melted chocolate over top and tap on table. Return to refrigerator until it hardens.

Peanut Butter Cream Center I

1   cup smooth peanut butter
1   cup confectioners sugar
½   cup margarine

Mix ingredients until well blended.

Peanut Butter Cream Center II

1   cup creamy white fondant
½   cup smooth peanut butter

Knead fondant until soft and smooth. Add peanut butter and stir until well blended.

Creamy Smooth Peanut Butter Cream III

4   ounces cream cheese
2   tablespoons margarine
10   ounces creamy peanut butter
1   teaspoon vanilla
1½   -2 cups confectioners sugar

Combine softened cream cheese, margarine, peanut butter, and vanilla until well blended; however, do not beat. Add enough confectioners sugar until candy becomes somewhat stiff; it should be moist enough to stick together when shaped into small balls.

Peanut Butter Creams IV

1 cup margarine or butter
½ cup peanut butter
½ cup light corn syrup
1½ pounds confectioners sugar

Soften butter with spoon on side of bowl. Add remaining ingredients and mix well.

Marshmallow Cups

Marshmallow ice cream topping
½ cup macaroon coconut
1 cup melted chocolate coating

Add coconut to chocolate coating and stir. Coat fluted paper cups or peanut butter cup mold with this mixture. Refrigerate until firm. Spoon marshmallow ice cream topping into hardened candy cups to within ⅛ inch of top. Cover with coconut-chocolate mixture. Tap on table and place in refrigerator until set.

For more detailed instructions, follow procedure for peanut butter cups (page 43).

Creamy Cups

1 cup melted white coating
½ cup creamy peanut butter
Peanut butter cream center recipe

Mix peanut butter with melted white coating until smooth and well blended. Using this, coat sides of peanut butter cup mold or fluted paper cups. Refrigerate until solid. Put peanut butter cream center in each hardened candy cavity. Cover with white chocolate mixture. For more detailed instructions, refer to peanut butter cup recipe (page 43).

Maple Cream Circles

1 cup creamy white fondant
½ teaspoon maple extract
Peanuts
Melted chocolate coating

Put two teaspoons of melted coating on a lightly greased cookie sheet. Tap several times on table to flatten to a thin layer. Put in freezer until set. Mix maple flavoring with fondant. Spoon a layer ¼ inch thick on hardened candy circles. Place approximately 15 peanut halves on top of fondant. Spoon on melted chocolate and spread to edges, sealing hardened candy.

Butter Cream Circles

1½ tablespoons soft butter
1½ tablespoons solid shortening
3 tablespoons light corn syrup
1 cup confectioners sugar
  Peanuts
  Melted chocolate flavored coating

Drop two teaspoons chocolate on a lightly oiled baking sheet. Refrigerate until firm. Mix butter, shortening, and corn syrup until blended. Stir in half of confectioners' sugar and mix well. Add remaining sugar and stir until smooth. Put a small amount of butter cream—¼ inch layer—on hardened candy circles. Top this with 15-20 peanut halves. Spoon melted chocolate over top and edges, sealing all sides.

Salty Krunch Bar

1 cup broken, salted pretzels
1 cup crunchy, puffed corn cereal
1 pound melted coating chocolate

Combine above ingredients in a bowl and stir. Pour into the candy bar mold which is ½ inch in depth.

Vanilla Wafer Dip

For a special after school treat, try this snack. Melt coating chocolate and dip vanilla wafers. This is done easiest by using ice tongs. Place a walnut or pecan half on top of each piece. Refrigerate until hardened.

Christmas Squares—Pecan Fruit Squares

1 pound melted white candy coating
1 can sweetened condensed milk
1 cup candied fruit pieces
1 cup pecan pieces

Combine above ingredients in a glass or pyrex dish 9" x 9". Mix together and press into bottom of dish. Cut and serve.

Crispy Sweets

  Vanilla sugar cookies
  Melted chocolate coating

Use cookies which have a sweet icing filling between two thin retangular wafers. Spread a layer of chocolate coating on top of a sugar cookie. Lay another cookie on top. Let set at room temperature until they are sealed together. Using ice tongs, dip entire cookie and place on greased cookie sheet. Set in freezer until they are hard.

Peanut Butter Raindrops

8 ounces melted candy
coating (vanilla or
chocolate flavored)

Add peanut butter to melted candy coating and stir until smooth. Drop by spoonfuls onto waxed paper. Set in refrigerator until firm.

Krispie Taffy Bars

1 cup sugar
¾ cup dark corn syrup
1 cup evaporated milk
¼ cup margarine
½ teaspoon vanilla

½ pound melted chocolate
coating
1 cup crispied rice cereal

Combine sugar, corn syrup, milk, and margarine in a saucepan. Stir and heat to 248°F. Remove from heat, add vanilla and pour onto a well-buttered cookie sheet. Set aside until cool, score into sections 1" x 3".

After taffy has cooled, combine chocolate and crispied rice cereal in a deep dish. Dip taffy pieces into chocolate mixture. Lay on waxed paper and refrigerate until hard.

Brown Sugar Candy

1 pound medium brown
sugar
⅛ teaspoon cream of tartar
½ cup water

Mix brown sugar, cream of tartar, and water in heavy saucepan. Stirring constantly, bring to boil and continue cooking to 236°F. Cool. Work with wooden spoon or spatula until candy becomes thick and creamy. Pour into clear plastic mold. Brown sugar candy is usually molded into the shape of a maple leaf or pilgrim boy or girl.

Maple Sugar Candy Leaves

1 cup maple sugar
⅓ cup water
2 tablespoons margarine

Cook sugar, water, and margarine in a heavy saucepan to 236°F. Remove from heat and stir until mixture begins to cool and thicken slightly. Pour into the leaf molds. Work quickly since candy sets up fast.

Fudge

Strawberry Fudge

Recipe can be adapted to other flavors by substituting other gelatin flavors, such as orange lime, or raspberry.

1½ **ounces dry strawberry
     gelatin dessert**
3   **cups sugar**
½   **cup margarine**
15 **ounces evaporated milk**
2   **cups marshmallow
     cream**
2   **cups chipped white can-
     dy coating**

Combine gelatin dessert, sugar, margarine and evaporated milk in a 3 quart saucepan and boil until mixture reaches a soft ball stage, 238°F. Remove from heat, add marshmallow cream and white candy coating. Stir vigorously until well blended. Pour into buttered pan.

Coconut Fudge

1   **cup chipped chocolate
     flavored coating**
4   **tablespoons margarine**
3   **tablespoons warm water**
1   **teaspoon vanilla**
3   **cups confectioners
     sugar**
    Dash of salt
1   **cup fine macaroom
     coconut**

Melt chocolate coating and margarine in top of double boiler. Add warm water and vanilla. Sift confectioners sugar and salt into bowl, add coconut. Stir in the melted ingredients. Press candy into a 9″ x 9″ pan.

Maple Cream Fudge

4   **cups medium brown
     sugar**
1   **can (13 ounces)
     evaporated milk**
½   **cup margarine**
2   **cups marshmallow
     cream**
1   **cup white candy coating**
1   **teaspoon maple extract**

Mix sugar, evaporated milk and margarine in heavy saucepan. Cook over medium heat to 238°F. Remove from heat; add marshmallow cream, white candy coating, and maple extract. Stir vigorously until well blended. Pour onto a buttered plate.

Dry Fondant Fudge

3	cups dry fondant
1	cup condensed milk
	Dash of salt
2	tablespoons margarine
1	tablespoon cocoa
1	teaspoon vanilla
½	cup chopped walnuts

Brown margarine until very dark, but not burnt. Mix dry fondant, cocoa, milk, and salt. Add slowly to browned margarine stirring constantly. Cook to 236°F. Add vanilla. Let stand until cold. Beat until creamy. Add nuts. Pour on-to buttered platter.

Bavarian Mint Fudge

2½	cups sugar
¼	cup margarine
¾	cup evaporated milk
2	cups marshmallow cream
½	teaspoon salt
½	teaspoon peppermint extract
1	pound semi-sweet chocolate coating

In a heavy saucepan, combine sugar, margarine, milk, marshmallow cream, and salt. Cook over medium heat until mixture starts to boil. Lower heat, continue boiling to 238°F, stirring continuosly to prevent candy from sticking. Remove from heat, add chocolate coating and peppermint extract. Stir thoroughly until smooth and well blended. Pour into buttered 9″ x 9″ baking pan.

Marzipan

M arzipan is a type of confection made basically from ground almonds. However some recipes substitute macaroon coconut and almond flavoring for almond paste.

Marzipan is easily recognized by its traditional miniature shapes of brightly colored fruits and vegetables. Shaping of pieces is usually done with fingers. To make fruits and vegetables appear more realistic, they are often coated with colored sugar, or glazed.

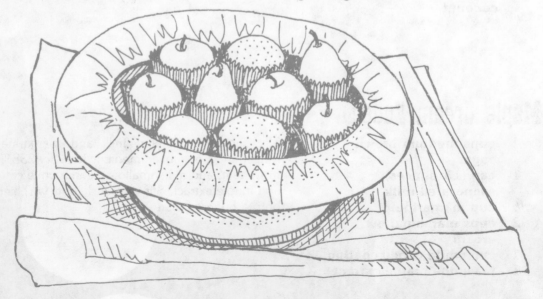

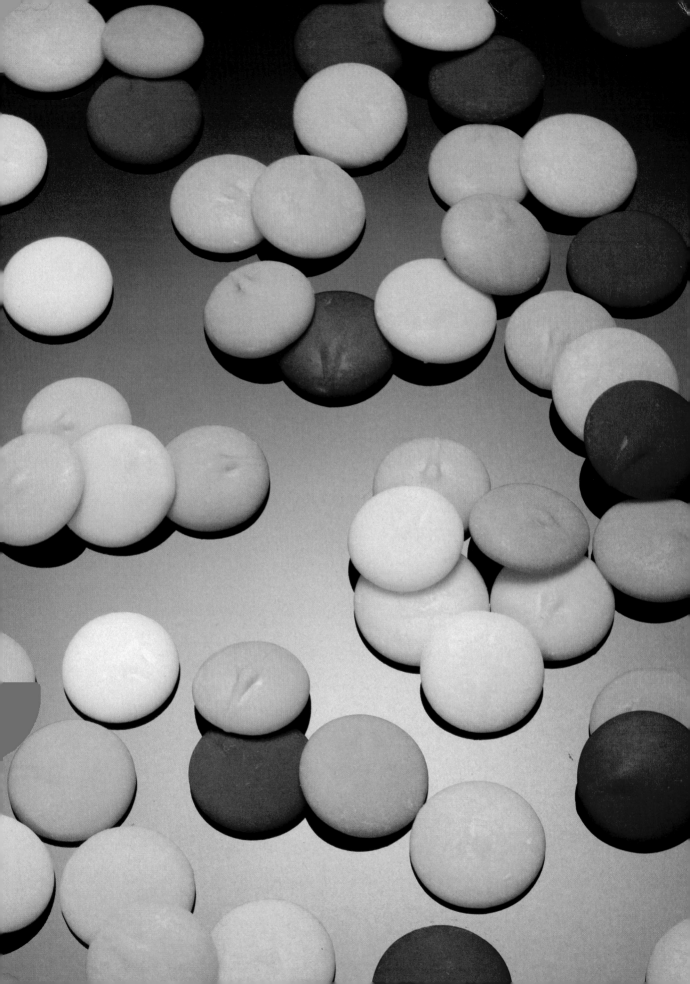

Marzipan I

- **3**   **ounces flavored gelatin**
- **2**   **tablespoons confectioners sugar**
- **2**   **cups fine macaroon coconut**
- **8**   **ounces sweetened, condensed milk**
- **1**   **tablespoon granulated sugar**
- **½**   **teaspoon almond extract**
    Plastic stems

Mix 2 tablespoons of the dry gelatin with confectioners sugar. Set aside.

Combine coconut, milk, granulated sugar, extract, and remaining gelatin. Shape into miniature fruits and vegetables. Roll in reserved dry gelatin and sugar mixture. Put plastic stem in top. Sometimes a clove is inserted in the bottom of certain pieces. such as: apples, pears, peppers, and oranges.

Marzipan II

- **1**   **cup almond paste**
- **1**   **cup creamy white fondant**
    confectioners sugar

Combine almond paste and fondant. Add enough confectioners sugar to make a stiff paste. Let set one hour. Divide into sections and color with paste food colors according to fruit or vegetable you intend to make. Shape into tiny fruits and vegetables. Let stand one hour. Paint on second color to accent certain areas as, for example, brushing red food color onto the side of a yellow peach. Let set one hour. Brush on glaze.

Marzipan III

- **7½**   **ounces sweetened, condensed milk**
- **2**   **cups fine macaroon coconut**
- **1**   **box (3 ounces) flavored gelatin***
    Colored sugar
    Plastic stems or leaves

Combine milk, coconut, and dry gelatin. Form shapes of fruits with hands. Roll in colored sugar and insert plastic stem.

*Use gelatin flavor which is the same as the fruit you wish to make. (I prefer this type of Marzipan made into strawberries; therefore, use strawberry gelatin.)

Marzipan IV

- **1**   **cup almond paste**
- **2**   **unbeaten egg whites**
- **1**   **pound confectioners sugar**
- **½**   **teaspoon vanilla**
    Paste food color
    Plastic stems

Combine almond paste, egg whites, sugar, and vanilla in a bowl. Let set one hour before using. If mixture still appears sticky, add a little more confectioners sugar. Work in coloring depending on color of fruit or vegetable you wish.

Shape approximately 1 teaspoon marzipan with hands into small fruits or vegetables. Place color accents by touching up with additional paste colors. For that natural appearance, insert plastic stems.

Almond Paste Molding

Add enough confectioners sugar to make the almond paste not feel sticky. Dip rubber mold into confectioners sugar and press in almond paste.

Marzipan Glaze

A hard candy glaze is usually applied to a piece of candy made from almond paste. After the almond paste marzipan has been shaped into tiny fruits and vegetables, make a glaze in which the marzipan will be dipped.

Marzipan Glaze I

1 **cup creamy white fondant**
¼ **cup water**

Combine fondant and water in heavy saucepan. Cook over very low heat until melted, raise heat to medium and cook to 270°F stirring constantly.

Dip each piece individually with ice tongs. Remove candy to a lightly greased cookie sheet and insert plastic marzipan stem immediately. Use glaze quickly for it will become hard. (If glaze is to be used over a longer period of time, set glaze over a pan of boiled water while using it.)

Marzipan Glaze II

1 **cup sugar**
⅓ **cup water**
Pinch of Cream of tartar

Using the top of a double boiler dissolve sugar in water, add cream of tartar. Cook until glaze boils and reaches 290°F. Remove from heat. Heat water in bottom of double boiler until it boils, and remove from heat. Set glaze pan over bottom of double boiler. Dip marzipan pieces and lay on a well-greased baking sheet. Insert stem at once.

As I Remember

Homemade Candy

Since nineteenth century cookbooks have very few candy recipes in them, I have concluded that candy just wasn't made by most homemakers until the turn of the century. And, then, old-time candy was hit-and-miss. Sometimes it got hard and sometimes it didn't. This was due to various reasons. One farmer's wife told me that her method of cooking was with a "Horse and a Hare". Similarly, Grandmother used to cook with the theory that two tablespoons was a hunk and a little bit more. Although we loved Grandmother very much, don't do as Grandma did—measure exactly.

Another reason for candy failure was that candy thermometers just weren't readily available then. Homemakers used a water testing method to tell if the candy was ready to pour. This is done by dropping a bit of the cooked candy off the end of a spoon into a cup of cold water. It's obvious that this method would only be somewhat reliable. The candy thermometer eliminated all the guess work in making candy, and even the amateur can now become a confectionist.

Make your homemade candy two weeks in advance and store in a wax paper lined tin can. Fudges, caramels, and fondants improve when stored in this manner. This tip seems to be just fine, but who can keep it this long!

Candy Testing-Temperature Chart

Type of Candy	Thermometer Reading	Cold Water Test
Fudges	234°F-238°F	Soft ball
Divinity, Caramels	245°F-250°F	Firm-ball
Taffy	260°F-270°F	Hard-ball
Homemade Marshmallows	275°F-290°F	Soft-crack
Hard candy, Peanut brittle	290°F-300°F	Hard-crack
Carmelized sugar	315°F-321°F	Carmelized

I always like to identify my recipes with my own personal feelings, and I have taken the liberty of sharing my own thoughts about testing candy with you here.

A **soft ball** is a round, soft ball that will flatten when taken out of the water and rubbed between the fingers.

A **firm ball** forms a definite round ball in water and will maintain its shape when held.

A **very firm ball** will not only form a round shape in water but is chewy if eaten after it has been cooled by the water.

A **hard ball** has been formed when a few drops of candy in water creates a hard, round ball that cannot be pushed together with your fingers.

A **soft crack** is when the syrup forms brittle threads when a little is tested in cold water.

A **hard crack** will make a noise when a little touches the water.

All about Fudges

Here are a few helpful hints on fudgemaking.

✔ Always use a heavy pan.

✔ Be sure sugar is dissolved before candy boils. Thus always start candy cooking over a low fire.

✔ Butter sides of pan to prevent candy from overflowing. This also helps eliminate candy from becoming sugary.

✔ To prevent grainy candy, try adding a little vinegar to the other ingredients. You will find it will become much creamier.

✔ For smoother and creamier fudge, add a teaspoon of cornstarch to each cup of sugar.

✔ To avoid burning candy drop three or four marbles into pan. Boiling keeps marbles in constant motion; it does most of the stirring for you. (This idea was garnered from an old-time candy maker, and I would not recommend it today. Many marbles are now made of plastic or other materials that cannot withstand high temperatures.)

The Fudge Doctor

Condition: fudge doesn't get thick. It is undercooked; therefore, return to heat and recook.

Condition: fudge gets hard in pan. It has been overcooked. Add a few tablespoons of milk and recook over low heat and stir until softened.

Fudge Variations
After fudge has been made and begins to thicken, stir in one or more of the following: chopped walnuts, pecans, or peanuts, peanut butter, raisins or coconut.

Fudges

Marshmallow Cocoa Fudge Balls

2	**cups sugar**
4	**tablespoons cocoa**
	Dash of salt
3	**tablespoons margarine**
1	**cup evaporated milk**
1	**cup marshmallow creme**
1	**teaspoon vanilla**
	Ground coconut

Mix sugar, cocoa, salt, and margarine in a large saucepan; add milk and stir until well blended. Cook, without stirring, over medium heat to soft balls stage (238°F). Remove from heat, pour into large bowl, add marshmallow creme and vanilla. Beat 2 minutes. Set aside, without stirring, 15 minutes. Beat at highest speed until stiff. Shape into balls, and roll in ground coconut.

10 Minute Microwave Fudge

Wow, what you can do with a microwave! Surprise your kids some night, walk into your kitchen to get a glass of water and return with a plate of homemade fudge.

3	**cups white sugar**
½	**cup margarine**
7½	**ounces evaporated milk**
12	**ounces semi-sweet chocolate chips**
7	**ounces marshmallow creme**
2	**teaspoons vanilla.**

Mix sugar, margarine, and milk in microwave ovenware. Put in microwave on Full Power or on High. Cook 6 minutes. Remove from oven and stir. Return to oven for 4 minutes. Remove and stir in chocolate chips, marshmallow creme, vanilla and nuts (optional). Pour onto lightly buttered baking sheet.

Economical Peanut Butter Fudge

Here's one that is easy to make and cheap, too!

2	**cups sugar**
1	**cup milk**
⅓	**cup peanut butter**
2	**teaspoons vanilla extract**

Cook sugar, milk and peanut butter to 245°F. Stir gently occasionally to prevent sticking. Add vanilla, cool 10 minutes, and beat at highest speed until creamy. Pour into lightly buttered platter.

Peanut Butter Fudge

2	**cups sugar**
	Dash of salt
¾	**cup milk**
¼	**cup light corn syrup**
4	**tablespoons peanut butter**
1	**tablespoon margarine**
½	**teaspoon vanilla**

Combine sugar, salt, milk, and corn syrup in a heavy saucepan; cook to a soft ball stage (242°F). Set aside 10 minutes; stir in peanut butter, margarine, and vanilla. Set aside for 10 minutes; beat until smooth. Pour into buttered pan.

Creamy Peanut Butter Fudge

2 cups sugar
1 tablespoon margarine
¾ cup evaporated milk
7 ounces marshmallow creme
1 cup peanut butter

Combine sugar, margarine, and milk in heavy saucepan and cook to soft ball stage (238°F). Remove from heat, add marshmallow creme and peanut butter. Stir vigorously. Pour into buttered 9-inch square pan.

Caramel Blond Fudge

1 teaspoon cornstarch
Dash of salt
2 cups sugar
7½ ounces evaporated milk
½ cup margarine
⅓ cup light corn syrup
1 teaspoon vinegar
1 teaspoon vanilla

Combine cornstarch, salt, and sugar in a heavy 2 quart saucepan. Add evaporated milk, margarine, corn syrup and vinegar. Cook and stir gently over low heat until sugar dissolves and mixture begins to boil. Continue to cook over medium heat to 238°F. Stir gently to prevent sticking while cooking candy. Remove from heat. Cool to room temperature. Add vanilla and beat until stiff, approximately 10 min.

Butterscotch Fudge Balls

Very, very sweet. Nice for display on a party tray with other candies.

6 ounces butterscotch chips
3 ounces softened cream cheese
1 cup confectioners sugar
Finely chopped walnuts

Melt butterscotch chips in top half of double boiler over hot water. Add to cream cheese. Add confectioners sugar until stiff (use more sugar if necessary). Form into 1 inch balls, and roll in finely chopped walnuts. Place in refrigerator until firm.

Walnut Fudge

2 cups sugar
½ cup milk
2 tablespoons light corn syrup
Dash of salt
2 tablespoons margarine
2 teaspoons vanilla
1 cup chopped walnuts

Cook sugar, milk, corn syrup, and salt in heavy saucepan over medium heat. Stir until sugar dissolves. Cook to soft ball stage (238°F). Remove from heat and add margarine. Do not stir. Let candy cool to room temperature. Add vanilla and beat until candy thickens. Add walnuts. Pour onto a buttered platter.

Velvet Fudge

Very rich flavor. Quick and easy to make.

2½ cups semi-sweet chocolate chips
14 ounces sweetened condensed milk
Dash of salt

Melt chocolate chips in top half of double boiler over hot water. Remove from heat. Add milk and salt. Stir until well blended. Spread into a 9-inch square buttered pan. Refrigerate until set. Cut in squares.

Cocoa Fudge

When making this recipe as a child, I just couldn't resist stirring continuously while cooking it; thus, the candy became very sugary. I'll never forget my dad eating it and proclaiming all the while what delicious fudge I had made. I realize now that it could only be love that prompted him to eat that candy—mistakes and all.

	Dash of salt
2½	tablespoons cocoa
2	cups sugar
1	cup milk
2	tablespoons butter
1	teaspoon vanilla

Mix salt, cocoa and sugar dry, add milk and butter; bring to boil. Continue boiling until soft ball stage is reached, stirring only when necessary to prevent sticking. This can be tested in cold water. Remove from heat and add vanilla. Allow to stand until lukewarm. Then beat until creamy and pour into buttered pan. Cut in squares when cool.

Cherry-Nut Fudge

3	cups sugar
4	tablespoons cherry gelatin, dry
	Dash of salt
¾	cup milk
½	cup evaporated milk
1	tablespoon light corn syrup
2	tablespoons margarine
1	teaspoon vanilla
½	cup chopped walnuts

Combine sugar, cherry gelatin, salt, milk, evaporated milk, and light corn syrup in a buttered 3-quart heavy saucepan. Bring mixture to boil, stirring constantly until sugar and gelatin dissolves. Cook without stirring until candy reaches 238°F over medium heat. Remove from heat. Add margarine and vanilla. Cool until warm. Stir in nuts and beat until candy loses its gloss. Pour into a buttered pan.

Rich Chocolate Fudge

Very sweet, similar to cake frosting

6	ounces semi-sweet chocolate chips
1½	cups confectioners sugar
2	tablespoons water
3	eggs
1	teaspoon vanilla
½	cup margarine

Melt chocolate chips in top half of double boiler over low heat. Beat melted chocolate chips, confectioners sugar and water at low speed until softened in a bowl. Add eggs, one at a time, and beat after each addition. Add softened margarine and vanilla. Continue to beat until smooth. Pour into buttered 9-inch square pan. Set in refrigerator and cool until firm.

Easy Marshmallow Fudge

2	cups sugar
1	cup evaporated milk
4	tablespoons margarine
16	large marshmallows
1	teaspoon vanilla
½	cup peanut butter
12	ounces semi-sweet chocolate chips

Combine sugar, evaporated milk, margarine and marshmallows in a heavy suacepan and bring to a boil. Cook to soft ball stage (240°F). This will take approximately 5 minutes. Remove from heat, add vanilla, butter and chocolate chips. Mix well. Place in buttered 9-inch square pan. Refrigerate until set.

Creamy Smooth Fudge

A great recipe. No one can mess this up. It's smooth and easy to make up. What more can you ask for!

4	cups sugar
13	ounces evaporated milk
½	cup margarine
12	ounces semi-sweet chocolate chips
8	ounces marshmallow creme
2	tablespoons margarine
1	teaspoon vanilla
¾	cup peanut butter (optional)

Mix sugar, milk, and margarine in a 4-quart pan, stirring often; cook to soft ball stage (238°F). Remove from heat, add chocolate chips, marshmallow creme, margarine and vanilla and peanut butter (optional). Stir until thickened. Pour on buttered cookie sheet.

Brown Sugar Fudge

Has a brown sugar taste that's sweet.

2	cups brown sugar
1	cup white sugar
½	cup dark corn syrup
1	cup Half-and-Half
¼	cup cocoa
2	tablespoons margarine
1	teaspoon vanilla

Combine sugars, corn syrup and Half-and-Half. Cook over low heat until boiling. Add cocoa and, stirring as little as possible, bring to the soft ball stage (238°F). Add margarine and vanilla without stirring. Cool to room temperature. Beat vigorously until thick and pour.

Skillet Fudge

Grandma often made this in her black cast iron skillet when we came to visit.

1	teaspoon corn starch
2	cups sugar
1	cup milk
2½	tablespoons cocoa
1	tablespoon margarine
¼	cup peanut butter
1	teaspoon vanilla

Mix together corn starch and sugar in heavy skillet; add milk and cocoa. Cook until a little dropped from a spoon forms a soft ball in a cup of cold water. Remove from heat; add margarine, peanut butter and vanilla.

Electric Skillet Fudge

This is the camper's special. Stir up a batch outside on the picnic table, using the external electrical hook-up for your electric skillet.

2½	cups sugar
	Dash of salt
½	cup margarine
1	cup evaporated milk
1	cup miniature marshmallows
¾	cup crunchy peanut butter
1	cup semisweet chocolate chips
1	teaspoon vanilla

Combine sugar, salt, margarine, and milk in large electric skillet. Set temperature control at 300°F. Bring to full boil and continue to cook for 6 minutes. Stir continuously to prevent sticking. Turn temperature control off; add marshmallows, peanut butter, chocolate chips and vanilla. Stir until well blended. Pour into lightly buttered pan.

Favorite Peanut Butter Fudge

1 cup white sugar
1 cup brown sugar
  Dash of salt
3 tablespoons margarine
1 cup evaporated milk
1 cup miniature marsh-
    mallows
1 cup peanut butter
1 teaspoon vanilla

Combine sugars, salt, margarine and milk in heavy saucepan and cook soft balls stage (238°F). Remove from heat and immediately add marshmallows and peanut butter. **Do not stir.** Cool to room temperature. Add vanilla. Stir pour into lightly buttered pan.

Cream Cheese Fudge

Good. Extra sweet—has powdered sugar taste.

½ cup semi-sweet
    chocolate chips
1 small package cream
    cheese (3 ounces)
1 tablespoon milk
2 cups confectioners
    sugar
1 teaspoon vanilla
½ cup chopped walnuts

Melt chocolate chips in double boiler. Remove double boiler from heat but let chocolate remain over hot water in double boiler. Set aside. Beat cream cheese with milk with electric mixer until softened. Slowly add confectioners sugar, vanilla, and walnuts. Mix only until well blended. Add melted chocolate and stir with wooden spoon. Press into 9-inch square pan.

Old Fashioned Fudge

This is the old-time fudge that sometimes got hard and sometimes didn't. Either way the taste is great! Try it.

1 teaspoon corn starch
  Dash of salt
1½ cups sugar
¼ cup light corn syrup
1 square (1 ounce)
    unsweetened chocolate
1 cup milk
¼ cup margarine
1 teaspoon vanilla

Combine corn starch, salt, sugar, corn syrup, chocolate and milk in a heavy saucepan and cook over low heat until well blended. Cook to 238°F, stirring frequently. Remove from heat and add margarine. Do not stir. Cool to room temperature. Add vanilla. Beat until firm. Pour onto buttered platter.

Christmas Fudge

You can get that Christmas spirit any time when you make this one.

2 cups sugar
1 cup Half-and-Half
¼ teaspoon salt
1 tablespoon margarine
1 teaspoon vanilla
4 ounces marshmallow
    creme
½ cup chopped candied
    red or green cherries
¼ cup chopped walnuts

Combine sugar, Half-and-Half, salt, and margarine in heavy saucepan only until sugar is dissolved. Stirring as little as possible, cook to soft ball stage (238°F). Remove from heat, stir in marshmallow creme and vanilla. Beat vigorously until candy starts to thicken and loses its gloss. Stir in cherries and nuts. Pour into a buttered 9-inch square pan.

Chocolate-Scotch Fudge

Here we have combined two flavors children like best and come up with one that's out of this world.

1½	cups firmly packed brown sugar
1½	cups white sugar
13	ounces evaporated milk
½	cup margarine
7	ounces marshmallow creme
6	ounces semi-sweet chocolate chips
6	ounces butterscotch chips
1	cup chopped walnuts
1	teaspoon vanilla

Combine in heavy saucepan sugars, milk and margarine. Bring to a boil over moderate heat. Stir frequently. Boil to soft ball stage (238°F), stirring occasionally. Remove from heat. Add the marshmallow creme, chocolate chips and butterscotch chips. Stir until smooth. Stir in the chopped walnuts and vanilla. Pour into a 9-inch square pan. Chill until firm.

Vinegar Fudge

The vinegar in this recipe gives it a smooth taste.

2	tablespoons margarine
2	cups sugar
	Dash of salt
½	teaspoon vinegar
2	tablespoons corn syrup
⅔	cup milk
¼	cup cocoa
1	teaspoon vanilla
½	cup nuts

Slightly brown margarine in heavy saucepan. Stir in sugar, salt, vinegar, corn syrup and milk. Cook over medium heat in covered pan until boiling. Add cocoa and increase heat to high. Cook until soft ball stage (238°F), stirring only when necessary. Remove from heat and cool to lukewarm. Add vanilla and beat vigorously until candy thickens. Stir in nuts and pour onto a lightly buttered platter.

Strawberry Fudge

2½	cups sugar
3	tablespoons dry strawberry gelatin
	Dash of salt
1	cup Half-and-Half
1	tablespoon light corn syrup
2	tablespoons margarine
1	tablespoon vanilla

Combine sugar, gelatin, salt, Half-and-Half, and corn syrup in heavy saucepan. Cook over low heat until sugar is completely dissolved and mixture starts to boil. Cook over medium heat, without stirring, until mixture reaches 232°F. Remove from heat. Add margarine and vanilla. **Do not stir.** Set aside until candy reaches room temperature. Beat until thick.

Divinity, Sea Foams and Penuche

Never-Fail Divinity

This recipe will be my friend for life. I have never made another divinity as good as this one!

2½ cups sugar
⅛ cup evaporated milk
⅓ cup water
¼ teaspoon salt
½ cup light corn syrup
2 egg whites, stiffly beaten
1 cup chopped nuts (if desired)

Combine sugar, milk, water, salt and corn syrup in pan. Stir thoroughly. Cook over medium heat, stirring continuously, until mixture boils and reaches a hard ball stage (252°F). Remove from heat, set aside while beating egg whites. Pour the syrup slowly over the eggs, beating continuously until candy starts to lose its gloss and begins to thicken. (Quickly stir in 1 cup chopped nuts, if desired.) Spoon onto wax paper.

Fruit Flavored Divinity

Make orange, strawberry, lime or lemon. I like to make this for a bake sale.

3 cups sugar
¾ cup water
¾ cup light corn syrup
2 egg whites
1 small pkg. (3 oz.) fruit-flavored gelatin
½ cup chopped nuts, optional

Mix together sugar, water and corn syrup. Cook to boiling, stirring continuously. Reduce heat and continue cooking without stirring until candy reaches hard ball stage (252°F). Set aside.

Beat egg whites until they are fluffy, add dry gelatin and continue beating until it holds a stiff peak. Pour cooked syrup slowly into egg whites. Continue beating at high speed until candy loses its gloss and starts to thicken. (Stir in ½ cup chopped nuts if desired.) Drop by heaping teaspoons onto wax paper.

Basic Sea Foam

Sea Foam is similar to Divinity; however, it's made with brown sugar.

2 cups light brown sugar
½ cup hot water
¼ cup dark corn syrup
¼ teaspoon salt
2 egg whites
1 teaspoon vanilla

Combine sugar, water, corn syrup, and salt in a heavy 2-quart saucepan. Cook over low heat until sugar dissolves and mixture starts to boil. Continue cooking, without stirring, over medium heat to hard ball stage (260°F). Remove from heat.

Beat egg whites until stiff. Slowly pour syrup mixture over egg whites and beat for approximately 3 minutes. Add vanilla and continue beating until candy loses its gloss and starts to thicken. Drop by spoonfuls onto wax paper.

Perfect Penuche

Another recipe handed down from Mother.

3½ cups brown sugar
¾ cup Half-and-Half
2 tablespoons butter
1 cup chopped walnuts
2 teaspoons vanilla

Combine sugar and Half-and-Half and cook to soft ball stage (238°F). Remove from heat and add butter. Cool without stirring, to 110°F. Beat until candy thickens and becomes creamy. Stir in nuts and vanilla. Pour into lightly buttered pan.

Basic Divinity Recipe

Here's another good recipe. With two great divinities—Never-Fail and Basic Divinity—you are bound to have the best candy in town.

2   cups sugar
     Dash of salt
½   cup light corn syrup
½   cup boiling water
2   egg whites
1   teaspoon vanilla

Combine sugar, salt, corn syrup, and water in heavy saucepan until sugar is completely dissolved. Cook until boiling without stirring until mixtures reaches a hard ball stage (252°F). Set aside. Beat egg whites until stiff peaks are formed. Using the highest mixer speed, slowly pour syrup over beaten egg whites; add vanilla. Continue beating until candy loses its gloss (approximately 5—7 minutes). Drop by heaping teaspoons onto waxed paper.

Chocolate Divinity. Melt 3 ounces semisweet chocolate chips in the top of a double boiler over medium heat. Set aside but do not remove top pan from double boiler.
 Make Basic Divinity or Never-Fall Divinity. After pouring the hot syrup over the egg whites, beat vigorously 2 minutes, then add melted chocolate chips. Continue beating until candy loses gloss. Spoon onto wax paper.

Coconut Divinity. Make Basic Divinity recipe. Add ½ cup flaked coconut when adding vanilla.

Rainbow Divinity. Make Basic Divinity recipe or No-Fail Divinity. After pouring hot syrup over egg white mixture, beat 5 minutes. Add ½ cup candied mix fruit and continue beating until candy loses its gloss.

Hints
1. Candy beats up fluffier if a large electric mixer is used in place of a hand mixer.
2. If divinity becomes too thick while beating, add a few drops of hot water.

Vinegar Sea Foam

     Dash of salt
2   cups dark brown sugar
1   cup water
1½   tablespoons vinegar
2   egg whites
2   teaspoons vanilla extract
1   cup chopped nuts

Combine salt, sugar, water, vinegar in heavy saucepan. Cook over low heat until sugar is completely dissolved. Continue cooking over medium heat, without stirring, to 250°F. Beat egg whites until stiff peaks form. Slowly pour cooked syrup mixture over egg whites and beat at highest speed of mixer for 3 minutes. Add vanilla and beat until candy stiffens (approximately 10 minutes). Add nuts and drop by spoonfuls onto wax paper.

Fondants

No-Cook Fondant

⅓ cup light corn syrup
⅓ cup softened butter (not margarine)
½ teaspoon salt
3½ cups confectioners sugar
1 teaspoon almond (or vanilla) extract

Combine all ingredients in large bowl and mix until well blended.

Fruit and Nut Fondant

2 cups white sugar
Dash white sugar
1 cup milk
1 teaspoon vanilla
½ cup mixed candied fruit
½ cup chopped nuts

Combine sugar, salt, and milk; mix until sugar dissolves. Cook, without stirring, until mixture reaches 238°F. Remove from heat. Cool to room temperature. Beat until creamy. Stir in vanilla, fruit and nuts. If candy isn't stiff enough to shape, add confectioners sugar.

Easter Egg Fondant

4 cups white sugar
1 cup water
1 cup light corn syrup
3 stiffly beaten egg whites
1 teaspoon vanilla

Combine sugar, water and syrup in heavy pan and cook over low heat until sugar dissolves. Continue to cook over medium heat to 240°F. Pour half over stiffly beaten egg whites. Continue to cook remaining syrup to 252°F. Beat egg whites for 2 minutes. Add vanilla flavoring. Pour remaining syrup over egg whites and beat until it can hold its shape in a ball.

Coconut Fondant. Stir (**do not beat**) 2 cups flaked coconut into the Easter Egg Fondant before pouring.

Simple Peanut Butter Fondant

So many peanut butter fondants, and all so good! Which one will you choose?

1½ cups confectioners sugar
½ cup creamy peanut butter
½ cup margarine

Combine above ingredients in a large bowl and mix until well blended.

No-Cook Peanut Butter Fondant

½   **cup margarine**
½   **cup chunky peanut butter**
¼   **cup light corn syrup**
1½   **cup confectioners sugar**
½   **cup crushed graham crackers**

Cream margarine in bowl until softened. Add remaining ingredients and mix well.

Cream Cheese Peanut Butter Fondant

3   **ounces cream cheese**
2   **tablespoons margarine**
1   **cup creamy peanut butter**
1   **teaspoon vanilla**
2   **cups confectioners sugar**

Combine cream cheese, margarine, peanut butter, and vanilla in large bowl and mix until softened and creamy. Do not beat. Add enough confectioners sugar until mixture can be shaped into small balls.

Creamy Peanut Butter Fondant

¼   **pound margarine**
¼   **cup solid vegetable shortening**
1   **teaspoon vanilla**
    Dash of salt
1½   **cups peanut butter**
3   **tablespoons milk**
2   **pounds confectioners sugar**

Combine ingredients in large bowl and mix well.

Buckeyes

½   **cup margarine**
½   **cup crunchy peanut butter**
½   **cup crisped rice cereal**
1½   **cups confectioners sugar**
    Melted coating chocolate

Mix all ingredients together in bowl until well blended. Dip in melted coating chocolate and cool in refrigerator until hardened.

Creamy White Fondant

Similar to the ready-made fondant you can buy commercially. This is a good basic fondant recipe that can be flavored and used for cream centers when dipping candy.

Follow recipe for Bonbon Glaze (page 75). Candy is ready to be used after it has "ripened" overnight. Omit instructions for dipping bonbons. If using extracts, ¼ teaspoon flavoring per half cup of fondant is used. Color with (water) liquid or paste food colors.

Chocolate Fondant

½ **cup margarine**
6 **ounces milk chocolate pudding mix (not instant)**
3 **cups confectioners sugar**
½ **teaspoon vanilla**

Combine margarine and pudding mix in a heavy saucepan and heat until melted; add milk and bring to a boil, stirring continuously. Continue to boil 2 minutes. Remove from heat, add sugar and vanilla. Stir until thickened.

Brittles and Hard Tacks

Microwave Peanut Brittle

Be sure to mix the soda in well, or you will get dark spots in your brittle.

¾ **cup light corn syrup**
1 **cup sugar**
1½ **cups salted peanuts**
1 **tablespoon butter**
1 **teaspoon baking soda**

Combine corn syrup and sugar in microwave cookware and put in microwave oven for 5 minutes, stirring during cooking process. Stir in peanuts and butter. Return to full power for 5 minutes, opening door only once to stir during cooking time. Remove from oven. Add soda; stir until well blended and foamy. Pour onto buttered cookie sheet. Let cool for 1 hour.

Electric Skillet Peanut Brittle

A golden-rod yellow brittle that tastes as good as it looks.

¾ **cup light corn syrup**
1 **cup sugar**
1 **tablespoon butter**
1½ **cups salted peanuts**
1 **teaspoon baking soda**

Combine corn syrup, sugar, and butter in an electric skillet and cook at 250°F until sugar is dissolved. Increase temperature control to 350°F and add peanuts. Continue to cook, stirring often to prevent sticking. When skillet temperature reaches 350°F, indicator light will go out. Turn heat control off. Add soda and stir vigorously until well blended. Pour onto a 9x12-inch lightly buttered pan.

Golden Peanut Brittle

1 **tablespoon butter (not margarine)**
1½ **cups raw peanuts**
¼ **teaspoon salt**
2½ **cups white sugar**
1 **teaspoon vanilla**

Melt butter over low heat; remove from heat, add peanuts and salt; set aside. Place sugar in heavy skillet over medium heat. Stir continuously until sugar caramelizes into brown sugar. Add vanilla. Stir peanut mixture into syrup. Pour onto buttered surface. Crack into small pieces when cool.

Light Peanut Brittle

2	cups sugar
¾	cup light corn syrup
½	cup water
1½	cup raw peanuts
¼	teaspoon salt
1	teaspoon baking soda

Combine sugar, syrup, and water in heavy saucepan. Boil to hard ball stage, 252°F. Stir in peanuts and continue to cook to 300°F. Remove from heat; add salt and soda. Stir vigorously to keep mixture from boiling over when adding soda. Stir only until well blended and then pour quickly onto a lightly buttered cookie sheet. Crack into pieces when cold.

Economical Peanut Brittle

Here's one for the thrifty homemaker.

2	cups white sugar
1	cup salted peanuts

Heat sugar in heavy skillet over slow fire until it caramelizes and turns clear. Add nuts and pour immediately onto a lightly greased cookie sheet. Break into small pieces when cold.

Butter Nut Crunch

¼	cup margarine
¼	cup butter
1	cup brown sugar
	Walnut or pecan pieces

Lightly butter platter. Sprinkle with nut pieces.
  Melt margarine and butter in heavy skillet; stir in sugar. Bring mixture to boil over medium heat. Then lower heat and cook slowly to hard crack stage, 300°F. This will take approximately 12 minutes. Pour onto prepared platter.

(Old-Time) Hard Candy

Granddad often had a jar of this in the living room. We weren't allowed to ask for a piece; so, we'd just sit, wish and watch that jar of candy until Granddad invited us to help ourselves.

3	cups sugar
1	cup water
¾	teaspoon cream of tartar
1	teaspoon oil flavoring

Combine sugar, water, and cream of tartar in heavy saucepan and heat to 300°F. Remove from heat, add flavoring (and coloring if desired). Stir and pour immediately onto a lightly greased cookie sheet. When cool, break into small pieces, dust with confectioners sugar and store in a jar.

Hard Candy Lollipops. Make one recipe (Old-Time) Hard Candy. After candy reaches 300°F remove from heat, stir in oil flavoring and food coloring. Drop by spoonfulls onto a greased cookie sheet. Lay sucker stick in place on each circle of candy. Spoon another layer of hot candy syrup over each piece.

Lollipops with a Mold. Molded suckers can be made by using a metal mold. Coat the mold with vegetable oil before using. Insert the rolled paper sucker stick into the cavity made for it. After candy reaches the required cooking temperature and flavoring has been added, pour it into the prepared mold. Do not attempt to touch or move the mold: it will be very hot. Let set until cool and turn upside down to release.

Christmas Hard Tack

Shiny pieces that are very pretty to look at and good tasting, too.

2 cups sugar
½ cup water
½ cup light corn syrup
1 teaspoon oil flavoring
food coloring

Combine sugar, water, and corn syrup in heavy saucepan, and cook to hard crack (310°F). Remove from heat. Add food coloring, then the flavoring. (I recommend adding the flavoring outdoors because the candy will vaporize somewhat. This leaves a very strong odor in the home.) Stir vigorously and pour at once onto a lightly greased cookie sheet.

Tiddly Winks. Make one batch Christmas Hard Tack. After candy reaches 310°F, divide into four pans, color each differently, and flavor each according to the color. Drop by teaspoons onto a lightly greased cookie sheet forming 1-inch round circles.

Horehound Candy

This recipe has been handed down for generations to be used for a nagging cough.

3 cups brown sugar
  pinch salt
½ cup light corn syrup
⅓ cup vinegar
⅓ cup water
2 tablespoon margarine
1 teaspoon vanilla
1 teaspoon horehound oil
  flavoring

Cook sugar, salt, corn syrup, vinegar, and water to hard ball stage (250°F). Add margarine and continue to cook to 310°F. Remove from heat, add vanilla and flavoring. Pour onto lightly greased baking pan.

Red Candy Apples

When the carnival came to town, Mother and Dad gave us each a dollar so we could get an all-day ticket. We sure did enjoy the rides, but even more, we liked the taste of those delicious red candy apples and cotton candy.

12 medium apples
   wooden skewers or ice
   cream sticks
2 cups sugar
1⅔ cups light corn syrup
⅔ cups water
   red food coloring

Wash apples, remove stems, and insert sticks in center. Lightly grease cookie sheet and set aside.

Mix sugar, corn syrup, and water in heavy saucepan. Place over low heat and stir until sugar dissolves. Continue to cook over medium heat, stirring as little as possible to prevent sticking. When candy reaches 300°F, remove from heat and add red food coloring. Carefully, dip apples into hot syrup; let excess drip against side of pan, and set on prepared cookie sheet.

Hot Cinnamon Apples. Follow recipe for Red Candy Apples. Add ½ teaspoon cinnamon oil flavoring after removing from heat. Continue to follow recipe as directed.

Butterscotch

Similar to brittle but has a lot more butter.

1	cup sugar
¼	cup light corn syrup
	dash salt
½	cup butter
1	tablespoon water
2	teaspoons vinegar

Combine above ingredients in heavy saucepan. Cook over medium heat, stirring until sugar dissolves. Reduce heat just so mixture continues to boil. Stir occasionally to prevent sticking. Cook to hard crack stage (300°F). Remove from heat and pour into buttered pan. Score into 1-inch squares; let harden and break apart.

Golden Butterscotch Rounds

These look like little gold pieces and kids really have a lot of fun with these.

2	cups sugar
½	cup light corn syrup
1½	cups water
½	cup butter
1	teaspoon vanilla

Combine sugar, syrup, and water in heavy saucepan. Stir only until sugar is dissolved. Cook to 275°F. Add butter and continue to cook to 300°F. Remove from heat; add vanilla. Drop by spoonfuls into lightly greased muffin tins.

Caramels, Taffies, Nougats

Easy Soft Caramels

This is not a caramel hard enough to cut; I use this one when making turtles.

1	can (14 oz.) sweetened condensed milk

Remove paper label and completely immerse unopened can of milk in a pan of water. Place over medium heat until water boils. Lower heat until water temperature is maintained just at boiling point. Continue to cook for five hours. Add boiling water as needed to keep the unopened can completely covered with water at all times. After required cooking time has elapsed, remove pan of water from heat. Cool canned milk in the cooking water until the water reaches room temperature. Milk, which has now caramelized, is ready for use.
Note: Several cans of milk can be prepared at a time.

Aunt Polly's Caramels

A great caramel recipe; has a mild, smooth taste and your results will be amazing.

2	cups sugar
1½	cups light corn syrup
2	cups evaporated milk
½	cup margarine
1	teaspoon vanilla

Combine sugar and corn syrup in heavy saucepan. Stir occasionally and heat to 300°F. Add evaporated milk and margarine. Stirring continuously, cook to 250°F. Remove from heat and add vanilla. Pour onto a lightly buttered baking sheet. Cut and wrap individually in wax paper.

Brown Sugar Caramel

No other caramels can compare with this taste.

- 1 **pound brown sugar**
- ¾ **cup butter**
- 1 **cup dark corn syrup**
- 1 **can (14 oz.) sweetened condensed milk**
- 1 **cup chopped nuts**
- 2 **teaspoons vanilla**

Place brown sugar, butter, corn syrup and milk in heavy saucepan and bring to boil over medium heat to hard ball stage (255°F). Remove from heat, add nuts and vanilla. Stir and pour into lightly buttered 9-inch square pan. Cool and cut into squares. Wrap individually in wax paper.

Golden Caramels

- 1⅓ **cup sugar**
- ⅓ **cup dark corn syrup**
- ⅛ **teaspoon cream of tartar**
- ⅔ **cup Half-and-Half**
- 2 **teaspoons vanilla**
- 1 **cup chopped nuts**
- 1 **tablespoon margarine**

Combine sugar, corn syrup, and cream of tartar in heavy saucepan. Bring to boil over medium heat. Slowly add Half-and-Half, stirring continuosly. Continue to cook to 250°F. Add vanilla, nuts and margarine. Mix well and pour onto a lightly greased pan. Cool and cut into squares. Wrap individually in wax paper.

Chocolate Caramel

- 1 **cup sugar**
- ¾ **cup light corn syrup**
  Dash of salt
- ¼ **cup cocoa**
- 2 **tablespoons margarine**
- 1½ **cup light cream**
- 1 **teaspoon vanilla**
- ¾ **cup chopped nuts**

Combine sugar, light corn syrup, salt, cocoa, margarine and ¾ cup light cream in heavy saucepan. Cook and stir over medium heat to soft ball stage (234°F). Add ¾ cup cream and boil again to 252°F, stirring continuously. Remove from heat; add vanilla and nuts. Stir immediately until well blended. Pour into buttered 9-inch square pan. Set aside until cold. Cut into squares and wrap individually in wax paper.

Caramel Apples

- 12 **medium cooking or eating apples**
- 1 **recipe Aunt Polly's Caramels (page 66)**

Clean apples and insert ice cream sticks or skewers. Cook caramel recipe only to 245°F. When finished simply dip apples instead of pouring candy onto a baking sheet.

Fast and Easy Caramel Apples

- ½ **pound store-bought caramels**
- 12 **apples and skewers**
- 2 **tablespoons milk**

Combine caramels and milk in top of double boiler over hot water. Stir until melted over low heat. Dip apples and set on greased cookie sheet.

Caramel Pinwheels

I remember unrolling the candy and eating all that sweet sugar center and saving the caramel part till last.

1   **recipe Aunt Polly's
     Caramels (page 66)**
1   **medium potato**
1   **pound confectioners
     sugar**
1   **teaspoon vanilla**

Cook potato with skin on until soft. Peel as soon as it is cool enough to handle. Place in blender and mash until softened. Add vanilla and enough confectioners sugar until the mixture becomes thick enough to spread. Set aside. Make recipe for Aunt Polly's Caramels but let it cook to 255°F. Pour onto a 10" x 13" greased cookie sheet. Let cool and spread with sugar mixture. Cut into thirds lengthwise. Roll small strips into pinwheels forming three 13-inch candy rolls. Slice ½ inch. Each roll will make approximately 25 pieces. Dust with confectioners sugar.

Caramel Turtles

12   **ounces milk chocolate
     chips**
6   **ounces pecan halfs**
1   **recipe Aunt Polly's
     Caramels (page 66)
     cooked to 245°F**

Melt chocolate chips in top of double boiler over low heat. Drop 20 spoonfuls of chocolate in individual piles on well-greased cookie sheet. Tap firmly on table so piles form a thin circle. Lay 3-4 pecans on each. Cool until firm. Spoon on soft caramel to within ½ inch from edge of candy piece. Spoon melted chocolate chips over each piece covering caramel and nuts. Cool until firm.

Salt Water Taffy

1   **cup sugar**
2   **tablespoon cornstarch**
½   **teaspoon salt**
½   **cup water**
¾   **cup light corn syrup**
2   **tablespoons margarine**
1   **teaspoon vanilla
     Food coloring**

Combine sugar and cornstarch in heavy saucepan. Add salt to water, then add this to sugar mixture; stir in corn syrup and add margarine. Cook over low heat, stirring continuously, until sugar is dissolved and mixture starts to boil. Continue to cook, without stirring, to 265°F. Remove from heat, add vanilla and pour into 3 individual buttered pans. Add a few drops of different colorings to each. Work with spatula until cool enough to handle. Butter hands and pull with fingertips until light and glossy. Cut with scissors dipped in hot water. Wrap indiviaually in wax paper.

Hot Cinnamon Taffy. Make one recipe Salt Water Taffy. Add ¼ teaspoon oil of Cinnamon and four drops red liquid food coloring to taffy immediately after pouing into pans. Continue as directed under Salt Water Taffy.

Butter Rum Taffy

Here's one that's really good!

2	cups sugar
	Dash of salt
1	cup light corn syrup
½	cup boiling water
1	tablespoon vinegar
2	tablespoons margarine
½	teaspoon butter rum extract

Combine sugar, salt, corn syrup, and water in a heavy saucepan. Stir over low heat and add vinegar and margarine. Continue to cook, stirring only occasionally until mixture reaches 265°F. Remove from heat and stir in butter rum extract. Pour into lightly buttered pan. With a heavy spatula, work candy from edges toward center. When cool enough to be handled, butter fingers and put candy between hands until it becomes hard to pull. Pull into a ½-inch diameter rope. Cut with scissors and wrap individually.

Molasses Taffy

1	cup brown sugar
	Dash of salt
¾	cup molasses
2	tablespoons butter
1	tablespoon vinegar

Combine above ingredients in heavy saucepan. Stir and cook over low heat until sugar is dissolved. Continue to cook, bringing to boil, over medium heat until mixture reaches 260°F. Pour into a large buttered pan. Work with spatula from edges toward center. When cool enough to handle, pull candy apart with hands until candy becomes light colored and hard to pull. Cut with scissors into 1-inch pieces. Wrap individually.

Chocolate Taffy

Very good! Similar to the candy bought at the grocery store and wrapped individually. We'd all dig through the bag to get the chocolate ones first—well, here it is.

1½	cups sugar
1	cup light corn syrup
3	tablespoons cocoa
1	cup Half-and-Half
¼	cup margarine
1	teaspoon vanilla

Combine sugar, corn syrup, cocoa, Half-and-Half and 2 tablespoons margarine in heavy saucepan. Cook over low heat until sugar dissolves. Continue cooking over medium heat to the hard ball stage (255°F). Stir only when necessary to prevent candy from boiling over. Remove from heat. Add vanilla and remaining margarine. Pour onto lightly buttered cookie sheet. Cool and cut into small squares. Wrap individually in wax paper.

Holiday Nougat

A smooth white nougat with fruit and nuts added. This is my favorite nougat recipe.

1 ½   **cups sugar**
½   **cup water**
¾   **cup light corn syrup**
¼   **cup white vegetable shortening**
3   **cups marshmallow creme**
½   **cup confectioners sugar**
1   **cup chopped pecans**
1   **cup candied fruit**

Combine sugar, water and corn syrup in heavy saucepan. Stir and cook over low heat until sugar dissolves and mixture starts to boil. Continue to cook over medium heat to 255°F. Remove from heat; cool to 175°F. Add vegetable shortening, marshmallow creme, beat for 5 minutes at highest speed. Stir in confectioners sugar. Stirring gently, add pecans and fruit. Pour into a lightly buttered pan. When cool, cut into squares and wrap individually in wax paper.

Creamy Golden Nougat

No gift box of confections is complete without this.

2   **cups sugar**
   Dash of salt
½   **cup light corn syrup**
⅓   **cup water**
1   **tablespoon margarine**
½   **cup Half-and-Half**
1   **teaspoon almond extract**
1   **cup pecan halves**
1   **cup mixed candied cherries**

Combine sugar, salt, corn syrup, and water in heavy saucepan. Stir well. Bring to a full boil over low heat, stirring only occasionally to prevent sticking. Continue cooking over medium heat to 275°F. Remove from heat. Add margarine and Half-and-Half. Return to fire and cook to 245°F. Cool to 150°F and add extract. Beat at low speed until golden and smooth. Stir in candied fruit and pecans. Pour into a lightly buttered 9-inch square pan. When candy is cool enough to handle, butter hands and knead until smooth. Work approximately 10 to 15 minutes, buttering hands as often as necessary to prevent candy from sticking to hands. Press into pan and place in refrigerator until hard. Cut and wrap individual pieces in wax paper.

Popcorn and Nuts

Delicious Caramel Corn

I make 18 quarts of this at a time. Be sure to take some to the beach or on picnics. It's something everyone likes and is cheap to make.

6   **quarts popped corn**
2   **cups brown sugar**
1   **cup margarine**
½   **cup light corn syrup**
   Dash of salt
½   **teaspoon baking soda**

Place popcorn in large, shallow pan and set aside. Combine brown sugar, margarine, corn syrup, and salt in a heavy 2-quart saucepan. Bring to boil over medium heat. Continue to cook 5 minutes. Remove from heat and add soda. Stir quickly to prevent overflowing. Pour syrup slowly over popcorn, stirring gently to be sure all kernels are covered. Bake for 20 minutes at 250°F. Remove from oven and stir gently. Return to oven and bake 25 minutes. Remove from oven and break apart gently.

Crazy Caramel Crunch

This candy coated popcorn has a mild taste of molasses; so, if molasses is your preference, you'll really go for this.

4	quarts popped corn
¼	cup molasses
1	tablespoon margarine
½	cup sugar
	Dash of salt
¼	cup water
2	tablespoons vinegar
¼	teaspoon baking soda

Combine molasses, margarine, sugar, salt, water and vinegar in heavy saucepan. Stir and cook over medium heat until mixture begins to boil. Continue to cook to hard crack or 310°F, stirring only occasionally. Remove from heat. Add soda, stir vigorously until well blended. Stirring gently, pour syrup over popcorn. Break apart when cool enough to handle.

Perfect Popcorn Balls

We never had a Christmas without these popcorn balls. Mother must have had a heart of gold and patience as strong as a wrought iron fence to let the nine of us butter our hands and help!

1	(10 ounce) package large marshmallows
½	cup margarine
8	quarts popped corn

Combine marshmallows and margarine in top half of double boiler over hot water; stir occasionally until melted. Cook 1 minute longer. Pour over 8 quarts popped corn. Butter hands; as soon as syrup is cool enough to handle, form into balls.

Popcorn Balls

Just like the ones Santa puts in your stocking on Christmas.

⅓	cup water
1	cup sugar
⅓	cup light corn syrup
4	tablespoons margarine
	Dash of salt
½	teaspoon vanilla
4	quarts popped corn

Combine water, sugar, syrup, margarine and salt in heavy saucepan. Cook over low heat until sugar dissolves. Continue cooking to hard ball stage (260°F). Remove from heat; add vanilla. Pour slowly over popped corn. Butter hands and shape popcorn into ball as soon as cool enough to handle. Wrap individually in wax paper or colored cellophane.

Colored Popcorn Balls. After making syrup for Perfect Popcorn Balls, stir in 5 drops liquid food coloring. Pour immediately over popped corn, stirring gently until it is evenly covered. Butter hands and shape popcorn into balls as soon as it is cool enough to handle.

Crispy Cereal Bars. Follow directions for melting marshmallows and margarine in Perfect Popcorn Balls recipe. Pour melted marshmallow mixture over 6 cups crisped rice cereal. Press into pan; cut into bars when cool.

Nuts

Sherry's Spice Nuts

While this cooks, it smells like you have a pumpkin pie baking in the oven.

1	**cup sugar**
	dash of salt
1/8	**teaspoon cream of tartar**
1/2	**teaspoon cinnamon**
1/2	**teaspoon nutmeg**
1/4	**teaspoon cloves**
1/2	**cup hot water**
2	**cups mixed nuts**
1	**teaspoon vanilla**

Combine sugar, salt, cream of tartar and spices in heavy saucepan. Add hot water and stir until dissolved. Over medium heat, cook in a covered pan to 245°F. Add nuts and let cool until lukewarm. Add vanilla and stir until creamy. Break nuts apart and lay on wax paper.

Maple Pralines

1	**cup maple syrup**
2	**cups confectioners sugar**
1/2	**cup evaporated milk**
	Dash salt
1	**tablespoon butter**
1 1/2	**cup broken pecans**
1	**teaspoon vanilla**

Combine maple syrup, sugar, evaporated milk, salt and butter in a heavy saucepan. Cook over low heat, stirring occasionally to 234°F. Remove from heat and add pecans and extract. Stir until cloudy. Drop from a tablespoon into paper-lined muffin pans, working rapidly.

Mallow-Minted Walnuts

1	**cup sugar**
1/2	**cup water**
1/4	**cup light corn syrup**
10	**marshmallows**
1/2	**teaspoon peppermint extract**
3	**cups walnut halves**

Combine sugar, water and corn syrup in heavy saucepan. Cook over medium heat, stirring constantly until mixture boils. Continue cooking to 236°F. Remove from heat; immediately add the marshmallows and peppermint extract. Stir until marshmallows are completely dissolved. Add walnut halves and stir until well coated. Turn mixture onto waxed paper and separate walnut halves.

Easy Peanut Clusters

3/4	**cup milk chocolate chips**
1/2	**cup salted peanuts**

Melt chocolate chips in top half of double boiler over hot water. Remove from heat and stir in peanuts. Drop in small mounds onto wax paper.

Candied Nuts

These sugar-coated nuts are somewhat sweet and really good.

- ¾ **cup brown sugar**
- ¾ **cup white sugar**
- ½ **cup sour cream**
- 1 **teaspoon vanilla**
- 2 **cups nuts—walnuts or pecans**

Butter sides of heavy saucepan and combine sugars and sour cream; stir over low heat until dissolved. Continue to cook over medium heat to soft ball stage (238°F). Remove from heat, add vanilla and stir until candy begins to thicken. Quickly stir in nuts, pour onto a well-buttered cookie sheet. Separate into individual pieces.

Rocky Road Candy

- 12 **ounces chocolate chips**
- ¼ **cup margarine**
- 2 **cups miniature marshmallows**
- 1 **cup chopped nuts**
- ½ **cup raisins**

Melt chocolate chips and margarine in top half of double boiler over hot water. Remove from heat. Stir in marshmallows, nuts, and raisins. Quickly spread in a lightly buttered pan. Refrigerate until firm.

Homemade Marshmallows

Try some in a cup of hot cocoa or just plain. They are light and have a taste that's out of this world.

- 2 **tablespoons dry gelatin (2 envelopes)**
- ½ **cup cold water**
- 2 **cups sugar**
- ¾ **cup light corn syrup**
- ½ **cup hot water**
- 2 **teaspoons clear vanilla**

Combine dry gelatin and cold water in bowl and set aside. Combine sugar, light corn syrup and hot water in a heavy saucepan and stir until well blended. Place over low heat and stir occasionally until sugar is dissolved and mixture begins to boil. Increase the heat; continue to cook, without stirring, to 245°F. Remove from heat. Slowly pour syrup in gelatin mixture, beating continuously. When candy begins to thicken, add vanilla; continue to beat until candy sticks in a clump. This mixing process will take at least 15 minutes. Pour into lightly buttered 9-inch square pan. Let set overnight. Mix equal parts of powdered sugar and corn starch in a small dish. Cut marshmallows and roll individually in sugar mixture.

Angel Wings. Make one recipe of Homemade Marshmallows. Layer chopped pecans in bottom of 9-inch square pan. After beating marshmallow and it has begun to thicken in bowl, spoon into prepared pecan pan. Let set until hardened. Cut into squares and turn out onto a board dusted with powdered sugar. Leaving the nut side as is, cover the other five sides with melted chocolate candy coating.

Marshmallow Coconut Squares

Like the toasted coconut marshmallows we sometimes bought at the Five-and-Ten-Cent store.

4   cups sugar
1   cup cold water
¼   teaspoon cream of tartar
3   tablespoons dry gelatin
    (3 envelopes)
1   cup cold water
¾   cup hot water
    toasted or colored
    coconut

Combine sugar, 1 cup cold water and cream of tartar in heavy saucepan and cook to 245°F. While this is cooking, combine gelatin, 1 cup cold water and hot water in bowl; mix well and set aside.

When cooking syrup reaches 245°F, slowly pour it into the gelatin mixture. Beat until mixture thickens, approximately 25 min. Pour into 9-inch squre pan which has been lightly dusted with confectioners sugar. Let set until hardened or overnight. Cut into squares and roll in toasted or colored coconut.

Coconut Pieces and Date Candy

Fast and Easy Bonbon Center

All the sweetness from the corn syrup is absorbed into the coconut, making them just like the bonbons you buy.

2   cups flaked coconut
½   cup light syrup
    Bonbon Glaze (page 75)

Place coconut in blender and chop into fine pieces. Put in bowl and set aside.

Place corn syrup in pan and heat just until it starts to boil a little around the edges. Remove from heat and pour over coconut. Stir and let set one hour. Form into small balls. Set in refrigerator until hardened. Dip in prepared Bonbon Glaze.

Creamy Delicious Bonbon Centers

2   pounds confectioners
    sugar
1   can (14 oz.) sweetened
    condensed milk
2   cups angel flake
    coconut
½   cup margarine
    Bonbon Glaze (page 75)

Mix above ingredients in large bowl and knead for five minutes. Shape into small balls and put in refrigerator to chill until firm. Dip into prepared Bonbon Glaze.

Date Drops

This recipe has chopped nuts and dates baked in meringue.

1   egg stiffly beaten
½   cup confectioners sugar
½   cup finely chopped nuts
¼   cup chopped dates

Slowly beat confectioners into stiff egg white. Stir in nuts and dates. Drop onto a lightly greased baking sheet; bake 300°F until lightly browned.

Bonbon Glaze

4   cups sugar
1   cup water
1/8 teaspoon cream of tartar

Wipe glass baking dish with cool, damp cloth. Place empty dish in refrigerator to chill until ready for use.

Combine sugar and water in heavy saucepan. Stir until sugar dissolves; add cream of tartar. Cook over medium heat in covered pan for five minutes. Remove lid and wipe sugar crystals from inside of pan with a damp cloth. Continue to cook to 238°F. Remove from heat and pour into pre-chilled dish, set aside until candy becomes lukewarm. Work with heavy spatula from edges towards center until candy becomes thick and creamy (approximately 10 minutes). Continue to knead with hands for three minutes. Place in air-tight container overnight.

To use as the shell for coconut bonbons, place small amount of glaze in top of double boiler over hot water. Heat over low temperature until melted. If too thick, add a few drops of hot water. Color a pastel shade using food coloring. Remove from heat but keep pan over hot water. Tip top pan to one side to make a "well"; this will give you a deeper area. Dip bonbon centers in glaze, rubbing off excess against side of pan. Lay on wax paper to dry.

Coconut Strawberries

1   pound angel flake
     coconut
1   can (14 oz.) sweetened
     condensed milk
2   (3 oz.) boxes dry
     strawberry flavored
     gelatin
     red sugar
     almond halves

Chop coconut in blender until fine. Combine sweetened condensed milk, coconut, and dry gelatin in bowl and mix well. Using approximately 2 tablespoons of mixture for each strawberry, shape with hands to resemble a strawberry. Roll in red sugar. Color almond halves with green liquid food coloring. Place two pieces on top of each strawberry for the stem.

Creamy Date Candy

This is really good candy that's easy to make and has just a slight taste of dates.

3   cups sugar
1/4 margarine
1 1/2 cups evaporated milk
7   oz. marshmallow creme
1   cup chopped dates
1   cup chopped walnuts

Mix and cook over low heat, sugar, margarine, and milk until mixture reaches soft ball stage (240°F). Remove from heat, add marshmallow cream and dates. Beat until creamy, set aside for 5 minutes. Stir in walnuts. Pour into a lightly buttered pan.

Mints

Creamy Cooked Mints

This is the kind that's smooth and melts in your mouth.

2 **cups sugar**
dash salt
1 **cup Half-and-Half**
1 **tablespoon margarine**
1 **teaspoon peppermint
extract**

Combine sugar, salt, Half-and-Half, and margarine in heavy saucepan. Cook and stir over low heat until sugar dissolves. Continue to cook, without stirring, to 220°F. Let set until lukewarm. Add peppermint extract; stir until candy becomes creamy and thickens. Pour out onto wax paper. Form into small balls and roll in granulated sugar. Press candy balls lightly with fork tines forming patties.

Sugar Mints

2 **cups sugar**
½ **cup water**
1 **tablespoon light corn
syrup**
8 **drops peppermint oil**

Combine sugar, water and corn syrup in double boiler; cook to 230°F without stirring. Remove from heat and double boiler. Add oil flavoring and a few drops food coloring if desired. Stir until candy becomes slightly thick and cloudy. Drop onto wax paper by teaspoonfuls.

If candy becomes too thick to make smooth drops, warm by putting the top pan over the hot water in the bottom of the double boiler and heat only if necessary.

Mint Patties

Bonbon glaze (page 75)
1 **teaspoon peppermint
extract**

Make one recipe for Bonbon Glaze. After it has ripened for 24 hours or more, melt in top half of double boiler over hot water. Add 1 teaspoon peppermint extract and coloring. Drop by teaspoons onto wax paper forming small patties.

Soft Buttermints

A no-cook mint that anyone can make with great success.

⅓ **cup softened butter**
⅓ **cup light corn syrup**
1 **pound confectioners
sugar**
1 **teaspoon peppermint
extract**
dash of salt

Combine above ingredients in a large bowl and stir until well blended. More confectioners sugar may be required to make candy stiff enough to form balls depending on the humidty. Roll in granulated sugar and flatten slightly with fork tines.

Storing, Packaging, and Selling

Storing

One of the finest qualities of homemade candy is its freshness. These delicious confections, therefore, should be consumed within two weeks after they have been made. However, keep in mind that some creams and cordials are perfected by permitting them to ripen a few days before using. Fudges, creams, and nougats should be placed, single-layered, in a wax paper lined tin can and stored in a cool dry place. Brittles and other hard candies should be stored separately from soft confections, because the moisture from the latter may cause the hard candies to become sticky. If properly wrapped, most candies and even popcorn balls can be frozen, thus preserving them for later use. Place candy in two plastic bags before freezing to prevent moisture from affecting the product. When ready to use, thaw candy at room temperature before removing from the bags in which they were frozen. Using the method outlined here, chocolates can be kept for several months.

Packaging

For that professional touch, individual pieces of candy should be placed in small fluted paper cups. This not only adds to the appearance but prevents the delicious morsels from bumping together. Boxes are available from candy supply shops. The one-piece plain box is recommended for clusters, barks, and hard tacks. However, the single-layer box (sometimes with a cellophane window on top) is the nicer selection. Chocolate-covered cherries or a variety box of chocolates packaged in this manner will prove your ability as a confectioner. Although boxes are classified as ½ lb., 1 lb. etc., a firmly packed pound box of chocolates doesn't necessarily hold a pound in actual weight. Approximately 25 pieces of candy will fit in a single-layer one pound box.

Cellophane Bags

Clear cellophane bags are available in sizes ranging from 3″ x 4″ to 6″ x 10″ . These are especially nice when packaging suckers. Most suckers will fit nicely into the 3″ x 4″ bag. Often, several ounces of clusters are packaged in cellophane bags, not only for appearance, but also to assure freshness. For example: 3½ ounces of clusters could nicely be packaged and sealed in a 3″ x 7″ bag. After putting the prepared candy in the bag, the bag can be sealed by using an iron preheated to the permanent press setting. Solid chocolate pieces, especially Easter items, should be packaged this way. Never staple shut any product containing edible substances. When the bag is opened there is the possibility that the staple will drop into the candy and be eaten.

Selling

Note: All local, state, and federal regulations must be observed concerning health laws, taxes and sales. Be sure to check with your authorities for these.

Two of the most important factors to consider when selling candy are cleanliness and neatness. There is the greatest temptation to lick the fingers when they get touched by chocolate. Always keep a clean damp cloth near the work area to be used for wiping hands. This will help to eliminate the problem. Also, work only with fresh chocolate which, when melted, becomes very smooth. If possible, when a piece of candy gets marked or bumped after it has been made, remelt it and make that piece again. Keep in mind that several clips are made on a 2-piece mold, thus no chocolate will seep through the edges. The more clips used, the neater the end result will be.

Probably the best-selling kind of candy is peanut clusters. The different types of barks are usually also readily saleable. Furthermore, these two items are easy and quick to make. Try to keep most of the items inexpensive. To accomplish this, it may be necessary to package only three or four ounces of candy in a cellophane bag to sell. The selection of sale items should not include more than ten varieties. It is not only difficult to prepare a large number of items but also confusing to those taking the orders.

Prices should be established on the basis of total cost and time required to make the finished product. As a general rule, double the cost of materials and ingredients. Be sure to include the cost of packaging. Extra charge should be added for items which are especially time-consuming, such as those that involve painting molds.

Index